FREE Test Taking Tips DVD Offer

To help us better serve you, we have developed a Test Taking Tips DVD that we would like to give you for FREE. **This DVD covers world-class test taking tips that you can use to be even more successful when you are taking your test.**

All that we ask is that you email us your feedback about your study guide. Please let us know what you thought about it – whether that is good, bad or indifferent.

To get your **FREE Test Taking Tips DVD**, email freedvd@studyguideteam.com with "FREE DVD" in the subject line and the following information in the body of the email:

a. The title of your study guide.

b. Your product rating on a scale of 1-5, with 5 being the highest rating.

c. Your feedback about the study guide. What did you think of it?

d. Your full name and shipping address to send your free DVD.

If you have any questions or concerns, please don't hesitate to contact us at freedvd@studyguideteam.com.

Thanks again!

Private Investigating Study Guide
Private Investigator Training Handbook and Practice Exam Questions [3rd Edition]

Joshua Rueda

Written and edited by TPB Publishing.

TPB Publishing is not associated with or endorsed by any official testing organization. TPB Publishing is a publisher of unofficial educational products. All test and organization names are trademarks of their respective owners. Content in this book is included for utilitarian purposes only and does not constitute an endorsement by TPB Publishing of any particular point of view.

Interested in buying more than 10 copies of our product? Contact us about bulk discounts:
bulkorders@studyguideteam.com

ISBN 13: 9781637753095
ISBN 10: 1637753098

Table of Contents

Quick Overview

As you draw closer to taking your exam, effective preparation becomes more and more important. Thankfully, you have this study guide to help you get ready. Use this guide to help keep your studying on track and refer to it often.

This study guide contains several key sections that will help you be successful on your exam. The guide contains tips for what you should do the night before and the day of the test. Also included are test-taking tips. Knowing the right information is not always enough. Many well-prepared test takers struggle with exams. These tips will help equip you to accurately read, assess, and answer test questions.

A large part of the guide is devoted to showing you what content to expect on the exam and to helping you better understand that content. In this guide are practice test questions so that you can see how well you have grasped the content. Then, answer explanations are provided so that you can understand why you missed certain questions.

Don't try to cram the night before you take your exam. This is not a wise strategy for a few reasons. First, your retention of the information will be low. Your time would be better used by reviewing information you already know rather than trying to learn a lot of new information. Second, you will likely become stressed as you try to gain a large amount of knowledge in a short amount of time. Third, you will be depriving yourself of sleep. So be sure to go to bed at a reasonable time the night before. Being well-rested helps you focus and remain calm.

Be sure to eat a substantial breakfast the morning of the exam. If you are taking the exam in the afternoon, be sure to have a good lunch as well. Being hungry is distracting and can make it difficult to focus. You have hopefully spent lots of time preparing for the exam. Don't let an empty stomach get in the way of success!

When travelling to the testing center, leave earlier than needed. That way, you have a buffer in case you experience any delays. This will help you remain calm and will keep you from missing your appointment time at the testing center.

Be sure to pace yourself during the exam. Don't try to rush through the exam. There is no need to risk performing poorly on the exam just so you can leave the testing center early. Allow yourself to use all of the allotted time if needed.

Remain positive while taking the exam even if you feel like you are performing poorly. Thinking about the content you should have mastered will not help you perform better on the exam.

Once the exam is complete, take some time to relax. Even if you feel that you need to take the exam again, you will be well served by some down time before you begin studying again. It's often easier to convince yourself to study if you know that it will come with a reward!

Test-Taking Strategies

1. Predicting the Answer

When you feel confident in your preparation for a multiple-choice test, try predicting the answer before reading the answer choices. This is especially useful on questions that test objective factual knowledge. By predicting the answer before reading the available choices, you eliminate the possibility that you will be distracted or led astray by an incorrect answer choice. You will feel more confident in your selection if you read the question, predict the answer, and then find your prediction among the answer choices. After using this strategy, be sure to still read all of the answer choices carefully and completely. If you feel unprepared, you should not attempt to predict the answers. This would be a waste of time and an opportunity for your mind to wander in the wrong direction.

2. Reading the Whole Question

Too often, test takers scan a multiple-choice question, recognize a few familiar words, and immediately jump to the answer choices. Test authors are aware of this common impatience, and they will sometimes prey upon it. For instance, a test author might subtly turn the question into a negative, or he or she might redirect the focus of the question right at the end. The only way to avoid falling into these traps is to read the entirety of the question carefully before reading the answer choices.

3. Looking for Wrong Answers

Long and complicated multiple-choice questions can be intimidating. One way to simplify a difficult multiple-choice question is to eliminate all of the answer choices that are clearly wrong. In most sets of answers, there will be at least one selection that can be dismissed right away. If the test is administered on paper, the test taker could draw a line through it to indicate that it may be ignored; otherwise, the test taker will have to perform this operation mentally or on scratch paper. In either case, once the obviously incorrect answers have been eliminated, the remaining choices may be considered. Sometimes identifying the clearly wrong answers will give the test taker some information about the correct answer. For instance, if one of the remaining answer choices is a direct opposite of one of the eliminated answer choices, it may well be the correct answer. The opposite of obviously wrong is obviously right! Of course, this is not always the case. Some answers are obviously incorrect simply because they are irrelevant to the question being asked. Still, identifying and eliminating some incorrect answer choices is a good way to simplify a multiple-choice question.

4. Don't Overanalyze

Anxious test takers often overanalyze questions. When you are nervous, your brain will often run wild, causing you to make associations and discover clues that don't actually exist. If you feel that this may be a problem for you, do whatever you can to slow down during the test. Try taking a deep breath or counting to ten. As you read and consider the question, restrict yourself to the particular words used by the author. Avoid thought tangents about what the author *really* meant, or what he or she was *trying* to say. The only things that matter on a multiple-choice test are the words that are actually in the question. You must avoid reading too much into a multiple-choice question, or supposing that the writer meant something other than what he or she wrote.

5. No Need for Panic

It is wise to learn as many strategies as possible before taking a multiple-choice test, but it is likely that you will come across a few questions for which you simply don't know the answer. In this situation, avoid panicking. Because most multiple-choice tests include dozens of questions, the relative value of a single wrong answer is small. As much as possible, you should compartmentalize each question on a multiple-choice test. In other words, you should not allow your feelings about one question to affect your success on the others. When you find a question that you either don't understand or don't know how to answer, just take a deep breath and do your best. Read the entire question slowly and carefully. Try rephrasing the question a couple of different ways. Then, read all of the answer choices carefully. After eliminating obviously wrong answers, make a selection and move on to the next question.

6. Confusing Answer Choices

When working on a difficult multiple-choice question, there may be a tendency to focus on the answer choices that are the easiest to understand. Many people, whether consciously or not, gravitate to the answer choices that require the least concentration, knowledge, and memory. This is a mistake. When you come across an answer choice that is confusing, you should give it extra attention. A question might be confusing because you do not know the subject matter to which it refers. If this is the case, don't eliminate the answer before you have affirmatively settled on another. When you come across an answer choice of this type, set it aside as you look at the remaining choices. If you can confidently assert that one of the other choices is correct, you can leave the confusing answer aside. Otherwise, you will need to take a moment to try to better understand the confusing answer choice. Rephrasing is one way to tease out the sense of a confusing answer choice.

7. Your First Instinct

Many people struggle with multiple-choice tests because they overthink the questions. If you have studied sufficiently for the test, you should be prepared to trust your first instinct once you have carefully and completely read the question and all of the answer choices. There is a great deal of research suggesting that the mind can come to the correct conclusion very quickly once it has obtained all of the relevant information. At times, it may seem to you as if your intuition is working faster even than your reasoning mind. This may in fact be true. The knowledge you obtain while studying may be retrieved from your subconscious before you have a chance to work out the associations that support it. Verify your instinct by working out the reasons that it should be trusted.

8. Key Words

Many test takers struggle with multiple-choice questions because they have poor reading comprehension skills. Quickly reading and understanding a multiple-choice question requires a mixture of skill and experience. To help with this, try jotting down a few key words and phrases on a piece of scrap paper. Doing this concentrates the process of reading and forces the mind to weigh the relative importance of the question's parts. In selecting words and phrases to write down, the test taker thinks about the question more deeply and carefully. This is especially true for multiple-choice questions that are preceded by a long prompt.

9. Subtle Negatives

One of the oldest tricks in the multiple-choice test writer's book is to subtly reverse the meaning of a question with a word like *not* or *except*. If you are not paying attention to each word in the question, you can easily be led astray by this trick. For instance, a common question format is, "Which of the following is...?" Obviously, if the question instead is, "Which of the following is not...?," then the answer will be quite different. Even worse, the test makers are aware of the potential for this mistake and will include one answer choice that would be correct if the question were not negated or reversed. A test taker who misses the reversal will find what he or she believes to be a correct answer and will be so confident that he or she will fail to reread the question and discover the original error. The only way to avoid this is to practice a wide variety of multiple-choice questions and to pay close attention to each and every word.

10. Reading Every Answer Choice

It may seem obvious, but you should always read every one of the answer choices! Too many test takers fall into the habit of scanning the question and assuming that they understand the question because they recognize a few key words. From there, they pick the first answer choice that answers the question they believe they have read. Test takers who read all of the answer choices might discover that one of the latter answer choices is actually *more* correct. Moreover, reading all of the answer choices can remind you of facts related to the question that can help you arrive at the correct answer. Sometimes, a misstatement or incorrect detail in one of the latter answer choices will trigger your memory of the subject and will enable you to find the right answer. Failing to read all of the answer choices is like not reading all of the items on a restaurant menu: you might miss out on the perfect choice.

11. Spot the Hedges

One of the keys to success on multiple-choice tests is paying close attention to every word. This is never truer than with words like almost, most, some, and sometimes. These words are called "hedges" because they indicate that a statement is not totally true or not true in every place and time. An absolute statement will contain no hedges, but in many subjects, the answers are not always straightforward or absolute. There are always exceptions to the rules in these subjects. For this reason, you should favor those multiple-choice questions that contain hedging language. The presence of qualifying words indicates that the author is taking special care with his or her words, which is certainly important when composing the right answer. After all, there are many ways to be wrong, but there is only one way to be right! For this reason, it is wise to avoid answers that are absolute when taking a multiple-choice test. An absolute answer is one that says things are either all one way or all another. They often include words like *every*, *always*, *best*, and *never*. If you are taking a multiple-choice test in a subject that doesn't lend itself to absolute answers, be on your guard if you see any of these words.

12. Long Answers

In many subject areas, the answers are not simple. As already mentioned, the right answer often requires hedges. Another common feature of the answers to a complex or subjective question are qualifying clauses, which are groups of words that subtly modify the meaning of the sentence. If the question or answer choice describes a rule to which there are exceptions or the subject matter is complicated, ambiguous, or confusing, the correct answer will require many words in order to be expressed clearly and accurately. In essence, you should not be deterred by answer choices that seem excessively long. Oftentimes, the author of the text will not be able to write the correct answer without

offering some qualifications and modifications. Your job is to read the answer choices thoroughly and completely and to select the one that most accurately and precisely answers the question.

13. Restating to Understand

Sometimes, a question on a multiple-choice test is difficult not because of what it asks but because of how it is written. If this is the case, restate the question or answer choice in different words. This process serves a couple of important purposes. First, it forces you to concentrate on the core of the question. In order to rephrase the question accurately, you have to understand it well. Rephrasing the question will concentrate your mind on the key words and ideas. Second, it will present the information to your mind in a fresh way. This process may trigger your memory and render some useful scrap of information picked up while studying.

14. True Statements

Sometimes an answer choice will be true in itself, but it does not answer the question. This is one of the main reasons why it is essential to read the question carefully and completely before proceeding to the answer choices. Too often, test takers skip ahead to the answer choices and look for true statements. Having found one of these, they are content to select it without reference to the question above. Obviously, this provides an easy way for test makers to play tricks. The savvy test taker will always read the entire question before turning to the answer choices. Then, having settled on a correct answer choice, he or she will refer to the original question and ensure that the selected answer is relevant. The mistake of choosing a correct-but-irrelevant answer choice is especially common on questions related to specific pieces of objective knowledge. A prepared test taker will have a wealth of factual knowledge at his or her disposal, and should not be careless in its application.

15. No Patterns

One of the more dangerous ideas that circulates about multiple-choice tests is that the correct answers tend to fall into patterns. These erroneous ideas range from a belief that B and C are the most common right answers, to the idea that an unprepared test-taker should answer "A-B-A-C-A-D-A-B-A." It cannot be emphasized enough that pattern-seeking of this type is exactly the WRONG way to approach a multiple-choice test. To begin with, it is highly unlikely that the test maker will plot the correct answers according to some predetermined pattern. The questions are scrambled and delivered in a random order. Furthermore, even if the test maker was following a pattern in the assignation of correct answers, there is no reason why the test taker would know which pattern he or she was using. Any attempt to discern a pattern in the answer choices is a waste of time and a distraction from the real work of taking the test. A test taker would be much better served by extra preparation before the test than by reliance on a pattern in the answers.

FREE DVD OFFER

Don't forget that doing well on your exam includes both understanding the test content and understanding how to use what you know to do well on the test. We offer a completely FREE Test Taking Tips DVD that covers world class test taking tips that you can use to be even more successful when you are taking your test.

All that we ask is that you email us your feedback about your study guide. To get your **FREE Test Taking Tips DVD**, email freedvd@studyguideteam.com with "FREE DVD" in the subject line and the following information in the body of the email:

- The title of your study guide.
- Your product rating on a scale of 1-5, with 5 being the highest rating.
- Your feedback about the study guide. What did you think of it?
- Your full name and shipping address to send your free DVD.

Introduction to Private Investigator Exams

Function of the Test

Most U.S. states require individuals to pass a test prior to serving as licensed private investigators. Each test is designed to assess the candidate's knowledge and experience in the field of private investigation. Requirements and tests vary from state to state. Candidates are tested on the laws and procedural responsibilities specific to the state where they are seeking employment. Exams are typically taken after the candidate files for a state license.

Test Administration

Each state's investigation and security board administers their own Private Investigator Licensing Exams. Test frequency, locations, cost, retesting guidelines, and rules related to students with disabilities vary from state to state. Most states give candidates a chance to retest if they don't pass on the first attempt.

Test Format

The private investigator test is typically multiple-choice and usually takes between two and three hours to complete. Dictionaries, books, or electronic resources of any kind are not permitted during the exam.

The test measures a candidate's knowledge of the rules and regulations required to fulfill the duties of a private investigator or operate a private investigative business in that state. Topics may include: state laws, federal laws, court systems, criminal procedures and due process, legal privacy requirements, criminal and civil law, private investigator restrictions, report preparation, and interpretation of legal documents. Specific information can be found via the licensing division website for each state: http://www.pimagazine.com/links/pi-license-requirements/.

Scoring

Since each state's investigation and security board administers their own Private Investigator Licensing Exams, scoring varies from state to state. Most require candidates to answer at least 70 percent of the questions correctly to get a passing score.

Recent/Future Developments

Because laws relating to private investigators often change and vary between states, candidates should check the private investigator test regulations in the state they wish to work.

Study Prep Plan for the Private Investigator Exam

1 **Schedule -** Use one of our study schedules below or come up with one of your own.

2 **Relax -** Test anxiety can hurt even the best students. There are many ways to reduce stress. Find the one that works best for you.

3 **Execute -** Once you have a good plan in place, be sure to stick to it.

One Week Study Schedule		
Day 1	Test-Taking Strategies
Day 2	Intro to the Private Investigator Exams
Day 3	Case & Testimony Presentation
Day 4	Case Management & Strategy
Day 5	Conducting Interviews & Research
Day 6	Evidence Collection
Day 7	Take Your Exam!

Two Week Study Schedule			
Day 1	Test-Taking Strategies	Day 8	Conducting Interviews
Day 2	Intro to the Private Investigator Exams	Day 9	Conducting Research
Day 3	Case & Testimony Presentation	Day 10	Practice Questions
Day 4	Practice Questions	Day 11	Evidence Collection
Day 5	Case Management	Day 12	Practice Questions
Day 6	Developing and Implementing Strategies	Day 13	(Study Break)
Day 7	Practice Questions	Day 14	Take Your Exam!

One Month Study Schedule					
Day 1	Test-Taking Strategies	Day 11	Attorney Misconduct	Day 21	Sources of Information
Day 2	Intro to the Private Investigator Exams	Day 12	Workplace Conflicts	Day 22	Access to Confidential Data
Day 3	Investigative Report	Day 13	Arbitration	Day 23	Practice Questions
Day 4	Types of Reports	Day 14	Mediation	Day 24	Review Answer Explanations
Day 5	Investigator's Notes	Day 15	Competent Investigations	Day 25	The 7 S's of Crime Scene Investigation
Day 6	Key Terms	Day 16	Efficient Time Management	Day 26	Chain of Custody
Day 7	Types of Evidence	Day 17	Practice Questions	Day 27	Forensic Science
Day 8	Legal Concepts	Day 18	Review Answer Explanations	Day 28	Practice Questions
Day 9	Practice Questions	Day 19	Interviews	Day 29	Review Answer Explanations
Day 10	Review Answer Explanations	Day 20	Methods of Obtaining Confessions	Day 30	Take Your Exam!

Case & Testimony Presentation

Introduction

A good private investigation report contains clear, concise facts and findings that are beneficial to the client. The report should not contain speculation, and if it contains third party or unverified information, it should indicate that. It should be very detailed and comprehensive. All leads should be exhausted and included in the summary. When writing a meaningful report, investigators should include those facts that are pertinent to the case.

When the private investigator (PI) reviews the report before submission to the client, it is imperative that he/she understand the client's expectations of the report. These expectations need to be discussed with the client upon accepting the case. The report should support the amount of work that the PI actually put into the investigation. The welfare and satisfaction of the client is the investigator's greatest priority.

Investigative Report

The investigator's report should be on business letterhead, with an attractive logo on top of the page. Marketing or public relations (PR) qualities conveyed through the investigator's report should not be minimized in value. An investigator's report should look appealing and professional.

The investigator's report could be the best marketing tool in the PI's sales tools arsenal. If the client thinks that the investigator did a great job on the case after he/she reads the report, then the client will likely use the same PI again, instead of hiring a different investigator.

Clients value photos; therefore, the investigator should include photos whenever possible. He or she should ensure that all photos have captions that explain what is visually depicted and what the relationship to the investigation is. Photos without captions could frustrate clients as they attempt to identify what the pictures represent.

Report Types

The PI must make a determination as to whether the occurrence under investigation is an *incident-based investigation* or an *accident investigation*.

An *incident* is an occurrence that is generated from an intentional act, and an **accident** is an occurrence that happens totally by chance. Private investigators work both incident cases and accident cases, and though the courts that hear these cases are different, the investigations are very similar. The investigator's job in both incident and accident cases will be to interview witnesses, take scene photos, make scene diagrams, obtain police reports, confer with lawyers and police, and speak with clients, whether the client is a person accused of a crime or a civil court claimant.

Report Writing

The investigator's report must contain the full scope of information pertinent to the case. The PI must include all relevant information regarding the case because what may seem trivial or unrelated to the PI might be essential information for the client.

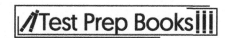

An investigator's report should be clear and to the point. It should contain relatively short, descriptive sentences and be concise overall. Lengthy sentences with unnecessary words can obscure important information.

It is incumbent upon the investigator to make certain that the facts in the report are accurate and verified. Information given with just one digit off in an investigation report could nullify a client's case and open the PI up to a lawsuit from the client.

Preparing an Investigation Report

The private investigator must write down all that comes to his or her mind immediately after the investigation, in addition to taking notes during the investigation. The investigator should start to prepare a report as soon as possible because the passage of time dulls a person's memories of a scene. Although the PI may have taken notes during the investigation, those notes should just supplement a report outline with the investigator's memory of the investigation.

After the investigator has written a rough draft of the report and produced a facts-driven outline, the investigator must, in consideration with the report, also include information from his or her investigative notes. Further, he or she should determine where pictures will be placed in the report and include descriptions in the captions for the pictures. Finally, the conclusion or summary should be included.

After the investigator completes the report outline, he or she should begin writing the final investigative report. Initially, a first draft should be written with an *executive summary* as the first paragraph of the report, which includes the general findings of the investigation. A very busy client will only read the executive summary, knowing that the rest of the report can be read at another time. The following example is an executive summary for a report:

Executive Summary: Investigation Report

On April 20, 2016 a signed statement was taken from Gladys Hernandez—45 years old, 5'3", 140lbs., black hair, neatly dressed in a blue pants suit, Hispanic, speaks with accent, residing at 554 W. 120th Street, New York, NY 10026, apartment 1138, telephone number 212-456-3456—regarding her eye-witness account of the accident that involved the Plaintiff, Manuel Montoya, on the sidewalk of 125th Street near Amsterdam Avenue.

The witness states she saw the Plaintiff trip and fall over the broken sidewalk defects on 125th Street, in front of 235 West 125th Street, Manhattan, NY (refer to diagram and pictures attached to this report). The witness also stated that she is familiar with this location and that the broken sidewalk has existed at the aforementioned location for over two years. The witness's signed statement is attached to this report.

After the investigator has placed the executive summary on the top of the report, other details can be added, and the report supplemented with pictures and diagrams.

Types of Reports

Surveillance Report

A major part of a private investigator's work might center on *surveillance*, the observation and reporting of a scene or *subject*—a person whom the investigator tracks over a period of time. Most of an investigator's surveillance time will be spent sitting in a vehicle with intensely-focused attention on the subject or scene. The investigator must maintain constant visual surveillance and may sometimes need to employ multiple persons for this task.

A *surveillance report* should be very detailed in its descriptions of people and physical actions. The PI's surveillance report should detail the time that notable actions take place. The following is an example of a surveillance report:

Surveillance Report

Date: 4/27/16

To: Colossal Insurance

From: Elephant Private Investigations

Claimant: John Johnson, residing at 34 Wayward Lane, Long Island Town, NY 11570

Location of Surveillance: In the vicinity of 34 Wayward Lane, Long Island Town, NY 11570

**Video and Photos Attached to this report

Date of Surveillance: 4/23/2016

Time Commenced: 6:00 a.m.

Discontinued: 9:00 a.m.

7:12 a.m.: I arrived in the vicinity of the Claimant's residence, 34 Wayward Lane, Long Island Town, NY 11570, a two-level red brick house, assumed a suitable position and commenced surveillance.

7:40 a.m.: The Claimant, John Johnson, (Caucasian male, 5'6", bald, 45 years of age, tattoos on left and right forearms) is observed walking out of the residence wearing work boots, jeans, and a blue-checkered flannel shirt rolled up to his elbows. The claimant is holding a shovel with a four-foot-long handle.

8:27 a.m.: The Claimant is observed digging holes with a shovel in a garden in front of the residence. The Claimant is observed using the shovel with both hands and throwing shovel loads of dirt into the side of the front yard. (Refer to photo #3 and video).

8:45 a.m.: The Claimant drops the shovel and answers his cell phone, after taking it out of his shirt pocket. The Claimant then runs into the residence with a free and unrestricted motion.

9:00 a.m.: Observing no further activity, surveillance is discontinued.

The usual header on top of the surveillance report with the executive summary should be omitted from this type of report. A separate note or informational report should precede the surveillance report and contain information as in other investigation reports, such as the executive summary, conclusions, and recommendations. A surveillance report is a strictly factual document. It relates the investigator's observations, plainly stating observations and events in chronological order. The PI may even reach out to the client from the scene of the surveillance, in order to gain authorization to continue or discontinue the surveillance.

PI reports—other than surveillance reports—have many commonalities: the reports will contain a heading, an executive summary, a main information body, conclusions, and possible recommendations. The reports should also have a case tracking number.

Arrest Reports

A private investigator has no more power than an ordinary citizen does when it comes to arresting someone for criminal activity. If a private investigator witnesses a crime, then he/she has no more power to arrest than an average citizen does. If the PI is acting as a bounty hunter and arresting a fugitive for a bail bondsman, then the PI has some arrest powers granted by law and contract, but the laws governing arrest vary from state to state. Great care should be taken if the PI decides to arrest someone because there will undoubtedly be legal and civil repercussions if the PI is guilty of false arrest.

If the private investigator does decide to arrest someone, then it is beneficial for him/her to document as much information related to the crime as possible, such as taking a picture of a weapon used or recording the perpetrator stealing merchandise. Moreover, immediate notification to police is incumbent upon the investigator. The sooner the police have taken charge of the criminal investigation and custody, the better the legal issues will turn out for the PI. A person is considered under arrest when he or she is no longer free to leave.

Security Department Review Reports

The private investigator will often be called upon to function in a security supervisory role. In this role, he/she will be responsible for the overall security of premises using security guards and other personnel working within the client's establishment. This kind of investigative assignment entails reporting on employee efficiency during security incidents or reporting on training exercises. The report also might detail loss of merchandise, suggestions for loss prevention of merchandise, or curtailing possible accidents by changing the physical nature of the premises for safer egress of customers and employees.

When the investigator is called upon to produce a Security Review Report, he/she must be very detailed in both the heading of the report, which would detail the date and time of an incident or accident, and the particulars of the occurrence. These particular facts in the report will be necessary because many different parties concerned with the occurrence/incident/accident will focus on details. The *who, when, what, where, why* and *how* questions will all need to be answered.

Daily Reports

Daily Reports are similar to Security Review Reports; however, a Daily Report may not detail any incident or accident. The Daily Report is a form detailing a security guard's observations and daily activities, such as checking that the fire extinguishers are in place and that the alarm systems are operational. The usual date and time should precede a short description of the guard's activity in a logbook, and the entries should be to the point and short in length. If an incident occurs, the officer should note on that daily log sheet that an incident occurred and that details can be found on the incident report that he/she will write.

Security Survey Report

A private investigator is frequently called upon to produce a Security Survey Report for a location. The premises must first be observed and evaluated. Many PI's use a template for the security evaluation. The investigation of the premises should focus on gaps in fencing, alarm systems, lighting, placement of security guards, procedures, and access of the premises by authorized personnel. The report should contain the usual header and executive summary. Then, in the conclusion, the investigator should focus on remedies for breaches uncovered that will improve the security of the premises. Photos and diagrams placed in the report are essential for demonstrating the investigator's observations.

Included in this type of the report are the investigator's opinions and recommendations. It will be incumbent upon the investigator to make improvements on the security of the premises through his/her opinions, regarding exactly what his client must implement in order to enhance the security of the premises. The PI can also recommend systems and options.

Bomb Search Reports

When working in a security role, the private investigator may be called to search for a bomb, if there was a bomb threat called into a facility. The private investigator must first know what a bomb might look like, and he/she must undergo training from a police, military, or demolitions expert before being placed within a facility that may receive a bomb threat. While it would be incumbent for the investigator to receive specialized training from an expert in order to recognize a bomb, there are a few obvious visual indicators of what a bomb might look like.

While completing the search, the investigator should not use electronic devices or radios, which could trigger the bomb frequency. Initially, he or she should be careful to look for anything that is obviously out of place, such as a backpack or a suitcase left in an unlikely location. If the private investigator notices a very large suitcase left on a stairwell, then he/she should immediately call the police. Other obvious indications of a bomb would be the observance of timers, fuses, or clusters of propane canisters. Bombs have also been known to be manufactured out of common household goods, such as aerosol cans and kitchen pressure cookers.

Whether the private investigator located a bomb or just completed a search for a bomb, the subsequent report to the client must include the following:

- Header with the date, time, and location of search

- Information on the source of the threat and if it was deemed credible

- A listing of the number of people evacuated from the facility

- Names and departments of police called to the scene

- A firm conclusion section at the end of the report that outlines whether any damage was incurred by the facility

- The names of people who may have sustained injuries and how they were medically treated and/or transported

Missing Person Report

The private investigator is often called into a security role when working for certain clients. When working for a school or, perhaps, a retirement home, the investigator is not only tasked with supplying security for a location, but he/she is also put in charge of the occupants of the premises. It is quite often the case that an occupant of the premises will go missing or be unaccounted for. In this case, the private investigator must formulate a very detailed report in order to assist the police and public—if it comes to the point where the person missing has not returned and authorities must take over the case.

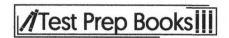

Important details in the private investigator's report must contain obvious facts, such as height, weight, skin tone, hair color, eye color, clothing worn, jewelry worn, shoe design, tattoos, birth marks or any other identifying detail that could help the police and other people searching for the missing person. The report should include the identity, the description, and all contact information attributed to the missing person, such as addresses and phone numbers of friends, relatives, teachers, and even contractors, such as cleaning people or maintenance people who may have had contact with the missing person. A recent photo should also be obtained.

The conclusion of the report must include the disposition of the case when the report is submitted to the client, detailing if the missing person was eventually found or if the police had taken over the investigation. Names of the police officers would also be listed in the conclusion of the report.

Property Reports

The private investigator is often placed into a retail setting as an undercover agent or a security analyst. If merchandise is missing or otherwise unaccounted for, it will be incumbent upon the PI to first assess what has been *possibly* stolen and provide a report to the victim (client) with a full detailed list, describing items that are deemed unaccounted for.

The Property Report starts with the usual header on top of the report, with the date and time that the report is being written, the location of the property loss, and the circumstances of how this report was generated. Details in the body of the report should include the following:

- The exact make, model, year of manufacture, and monetary worth of the property
- Any other details of the missing property
- A numbered list of each item missing
- The name of the property, along with the details

Any witness statements to the report should be attached, and the complainant should sign the bottom of the report, below the statement, which should include when the property was first noticed missing from its normal place.

Detailed Property Reports are important for insurance companies when honoring claims; therefore, the private investigator must make sure to satisfy the requirement threshold of facts in order for the victim to make an insurance claim. The PI may also be required to interview employees with jobs that may have exposed them to the areas or items that are missing.

Traffic Reports

The private investigator may sometimes act in a security role for a client and monitor traffic in a busy parking lot. Frequently, motorists violate traffic laws or cause accidents while driving in a parking lot.

In this setting, the private investigator should detail the parties involved in the accident by asking for their driver's licenses and registrations. The date and time of the accidents should be written in the header of the report, with the information regarding whether the private investigator witnessed or did not witness the accident. Pictures of the damage, in addition to pictures of the scene of the accident are important. A diagram showing the motion of the cars within the scene is also an important addition in a Traffic Report. If it is a private parking lot, police may not patrol it to enforce regulations, unless a crime has been committed. A PI can lawfully ask a person to leave a private parking lot.

If the private investigator is placed in a high traffic area with many accidents/incidents, then a logbook is also an important factor for each individual accident/incident report. Entering the log number on the individual report will help him/her keep track of any traffic trends within the scene that would be of interest to the client.

Offense Reports

If the private investigator is operating in a retail store as a security guard, there will be instances where a perpetrator has been apprehended. Nightclubs and festival venues are places where the private investigator will work in a security role. Fights, verbal abuse, and drug possession issues are incidents that often take place in these venues, and it is the duty of the private investigator to write a report on any incident where the client has specified a desire to know the details. Moreover, if the police are called to the scene, then the Offense Report will be important as information for subsequent criminal prosecution.

The Offense Report must include the date and time of offense, in addition to its exact location. The nature of the offense should be in the body of the report, with a complete description of the offense committed and the complete identity—including home address and date of birth—of the perpetrator and any victims. Any injuries should be noted, and any video of the event should be preserved for future use.

Where applicable, the PI should obtain pictures of injuries and draw a diagram of the scene and attach those to the Offense Report.

Victim Find Notification Report

The need often arises for the PI to provide security of premises or a venue where a social gathering occurs. The private investigator will be entrusted with overseeing the safety and security of a location and the guests who occupy said location. Occasionally, there is a victim of an accident or incident who cannot notify others of his or her plight, due to an inability to communicate because of injury.

If the person is injured, emergency medical personnel must be notified immediately. The investigator should attempt to obtain the victim's identity once the medical personnel arrive at the scene. It is imperative that the private investigator obtain the identity of the reporting medical personnel, where they originated from, and the make and model of their vehicles at the scene. Pictures of the victim and the events that followed once the victim was found should be obtained. The investigator should interview any witnesses present at the scene or anyone who can identify the victim.

If the victim is deceased, then he or she might be found by a passerby or the private investigator. With a deceased victim, it is important to identify the injuries that the victim succumbed to and write those observations into the Victim Find Notification Report. Additionally, the investigator should take a written note or, if possible, a video and audio record of any dying statements made by the victim as these statements would hold weight in court and are admissible. The identities of all police personnel that arrive at the scene should be listed. The PI should also obtain the criminal complaint number for future reference.

Traffic Accident Reports

Traffic accidents are commonly within the jurisdiction of the police; however, an investigator's duties required on a premises while performing security might entail obtaining all the information regarding a

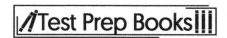

traffic accident that occurred on the premises. The Traffic Accident Report should include the following details:

- Identifying information of all involved parties, including, but not limited to, driver's license information, name, date of birth, and address

- Vehicle registration information, VIN number, make and model

- Insurance company information

- Pictures of damage to the vehicles, injuries, driver's licenses, license plates, scenes of accidents, and any other pictures the investigator can take

- Diagrams

Witness statements should be taken immediately at the scene. A traffic accident is usually a contested event between the parties involved, with each party claiming the right-of-way. A signed, objective witness statement is a powerful tool for an insurance company in their decision on how to handle an auto claim.

Workplace Investigation Report

Employee theft and misfeasance is a constant problem for employers. A private investigator will sometimes investigate the employees of a business for the employer. This investigation is also referred to as a *pen and pencil investigation* because when the investigator asks the employee questions, the investigator then writes down the manner in which the employee answered.

The employer first briefs the private investigator of the problem in the business, such as fraud or theft. Then, the employer or manager will provide details of the problem in the workplace and perhaps inform the investigator of who is suspect within the company.

The investigation will entail interviewing employees who have acted suspiciously, according to the employer. The investigator should suggest to the employer that those employees who may not be suspect but are in the vicinity of where the questionable occurrences have taken place, should be interviewed. It is sometimes the case where the least suspicious person is committing the most crime.

The Workplace Investigation Report should begin with the header of date, time of report, time of employee interviews, and all those interviewed. The following details should be included:

- The employees' exact names, positions, and times of their work shifts

- Detailed descriptions of what employees said in the interviews

- Any video or audio recording of the employee, if video and audio recording is authorized by the employer/client

At the end of the report, conclusions or suggestions should be entered that are pertinent to the case, along with any supporting documents produced during the investigation.

Investigator's Notes

The notes jotted down on a piece of paper by a private investigator can be introduced as evidence in court. Private investigation notes are also an important start to implementing a final report. Qualifying observations through notes on paper is the key to writing successful reports when describing an investigation location and the facts needed by the client.

If the PI cannot take notes while present at the scene of the investigation, then it is important that he/she write notes soon after leaving the location. The longer the private investigator waits to jot down notes on paper, the more likely it will be that essential facts will be forgotten, due to the passage of time infringing on acute recollections. The notes must adhere to what the client is looking for—in other words, those facts that are important to the case.

The private investigator must pay attention and immediately write down the date and time, and then continue with essential facts that detail exact scene location, correct spelling of names, correct license plate numbers, locations of possible witnesses, and anything else that should be mentioned in the final investigation report.

Note Taking

Private investigation is similar to news reporting as both professions follow the common method of documenting information with the six categories of explaining an occurrence: *Who, What, Where, When, Why,* and *How.*

- Who references the person or people involved in the investigation

    o Example: "Phillip Calderon and Ronald Sanchez, the superintendents of the building (hereafter referred to as the Subjects), were observed by the witness outside the apartment door."

- What references the circumstances and the reasons for the crime or accident

    o Example: "There was a gas leak somewhere in the building, and the superintendents didn't know where the gas was emanating from."

- Where references the location of the incident/accident and the location of where the subject of the report is taking place.

    o Example: "The gas was leaking from apartment 3D, at 2345 Rosedale Avenue, Bronx, NY. The superintendents entered apartment 3D, looking for which pipe was leaking gas."

- When references the time and date that the accident/incident occurred

    o Example: "At 2:45 pm, on April 17, 2016, there was an explosion in apartment 3D."

- Why references the reason for the occurrence or the motive of a crime/incident

  - Example: "The explosion in apartment 3D occurred because there was a buildup of gas from a leaking stovepipe."

- How references the circumstances that enabled the accident/incident to take place

  - Example: "The buildup of gas was facilitated by the windows in the apartment remaining closed and the superintendents checking for gas leaks by using a cigarette lighter inside of the apartment, hence, igniting the built-up gas."

Styles

There are three basic styles of note taking and report writing that the private investigator may use: Narrative, Question and Answer, and Chronological.

The *Narrative Style* is a very descriptive style and is often used when many details are essential for the report. It is written in the investigator's own words and can use the vernacular or quotes from other people referenced in the report, such as a person who was interviewed. The narrative style is the most time-consuming style, but it offers the investigator a means to present the most information in the final investigation report.

The *Question-and-Answer Style* is a set of prearranged questions that elicit specific answers. The advantages to this style are that no question is missed, since it is already on a form, and the information is obtained quickly. However, while the Question-and-Answer style is an efficient way to obtain information, it does not allow for any information that exceeds the set question boundaries; therefore, the client receiving the final report might not get the entire scope of information that exists surrounding the case.

The *Chronological Style* is used to document a timeline of investigation. Time-related information in a linear fashion is essential when taking notes and formulating a final surveillance report. Most surveillance reports are written in this fashion to highlight the time of events and non-events.

Computerized Report Writing

Computerized Report Writing has been recently implemented and has the advantage of enhancing a report's legibility and completeness of information disseminated. This type of assistance from a computer allows the investigator to write a report in a shorter amount of time using a template, while also accessing computer databases with links. This assistance from the computer should always be scrutinized for accuracy when the investigator is finished writing a report, due to the probability of cutting and pasting information between reports.

Preformatted Reports

Preformatted Reports facilitate the management of cases and enhance the flow of information in a busy investigation office by containing predetermined boundaries set within the report. The defining of information by lined borders in a report makes reading the report easier, especially when the investigator is conferring with other people in a meeting environment. If multiple people are looking at the same information in a room, this tends to facilitate conversation about a case.

There are usually five different types of preformatted reports used in case management: Incident/Accident Reports, Follow-up Reports, Property Reports, Lab Reports, and Supervisory Reports.

Incident/Accident Preformatted Reports are the most common preformatted reports used for writing and viewing information on a case. The report has spaces for details, such as time, date, and location of occurrence, along with witness information and identification of all parties involved in the case. Police reports are usually preformatted, so the officer can write down a lot of information in a short amount of time.

Follow-up Reports document each part of the investigation of a case. This type of report confirms that witnesses were interviewed and that photos were taken. The Follow-up Report verifies that investigators handled the sections of a case that were important for the final report.

Property Reports are very important because they list what items were seized or acquired during an investigation. It is imperative that property reports be detailed in the description of the items section, and the Property Report must explicitly describe who had control of the property items and where they were placed, for further scrutiny in the future.

Lab Reports detail the findings of a technician who may have worked with a piece of evidence. The report highlights what the lab technician worked with and the results of his or her findings.

Supervisory Review Reports include decisions to complete the case or keep the case open for further investigation. If the case is kept open, the investigative supervisor will detail recommendations regarding how the field investigator should proceed with the investigation of the case.

Key Terms

Indictment and Arraignment

Criminal cases can be a large part of a private investigator's work. Public Defender attorneys and private attorneys who specialize in criminal defense will frequently hire a private investigator to obtain any evidence that might help exonerate their clients of criminal charges.

When a grand jury is convened by a district attorney, otherwise known as the prosecutor, the grand jury will decide to indict or not indict a person with charges. A preliminary hearing might be called by a judge at any time, in order to ascertain the validity of the charges against the defendant. The judge will determine if there is probable cause to charge the suspect. A district attorney may also file a charge or complaint with the court accusing the defendant of committing a crime.

An *arraignment* is a formal reading of the crime that the defendant is accused of committing; it takes place after a grand jury or district attorney has made an indictment. The arraignment is held in court with the person accused of the crime—the defendant—present in the courtroom. The defendant's criminal defense attorney is also usually present. A private investigator working for the criminal defense attorney might also be present in the courtroom. The judge will set a bail condition, remand the individual, or release the defendant on his/her own recognizance.

After the charges are read, the accused states or pleads that he/she is *guilty* or *not guilty*. If the accused pleads *not guilty,* a trial date is usually put on the court's calendar.

Entrapment

When a person is induced or persuaded to commit a crime that he/she would not have ordinarily have taken part in, it is referred to as *entrapment*. Law enforcement would be guilty of entrapment if they were to set the person up—intentionally formulate events surrounding the person that expose him/her

to criminal prosecution—whereas if the person was otherwise left alone, he/she would not have participated in a crime.

A defendant who claims entrapment must prove that there was no disposition or intent on his or her part to commit a crime.

Totality of Circumstances and Bright Line Standards

The *Totality of Circumstances Standard* refers to decisions made by encompassing all the factors, facts, and circumstances in a case. In the final decision made, it is not just one factor influencing that decision, but many different issues and factors. A precedent in case law is also one of the elements in determining a final decision.

A *Bright Line Standard* is a single factor that determines if there is probable cause for a decision or an arrest.

Modus Operandi

Modus Operandi (MO) is a term that originates in Latin in legal parlance. It is a term used when defining someone's method of operation or the way an individual or group does things in a characteristic way. When speaking in investigative terms, a criminal's certain way of doing things shows a discernable pattern in methods and operation. Police departments usually keep an MO record in order to identify and track certain criminals.

Preparing and Presenting Testimony

Courtroom Appearance and Conduct

It is essential for the private investigator to dress professionally in business attire when entering the courthouse on official business—a suit and tie for men and a dress suit for women. A private investigator might be called up to the stand unexpectedly, perhaps because the opposing side in a case observed the private investigator in the building and decided to call him up to the stand. It is always better to be dressed professionally when giving testimony that should be convincing enough to help the client.

When speaking with attorneys, witnesses, and clients it is imperative that the investigator does not permit his/her lips to be read or his/her voice overheard as there will be opposing parties in the courthouse who will try to get close and listen to the conversation. These parties may try to read lips in order to get an advantage in the case or to glean confidential information from conversations and reading body language.

If a person attempts to elicit political or biased opinions from the private investigator, he/she should not cooperate with the person while in the courthouse. The opposing side involved in the private investigator's case will strive to achieve any advantage they can.

The private investigator must allow plenty of travel time in order to be on time for the trial. If the PI is not familiar with the courthouse, he/she should arrive early, so the layout of the courthouse can become familiar and to accommodate any last-minute courtroom changes. It may also be prudent for the investigator to make an advance trip the day before.

The PI must be conscious of maintaining a good attitude and remaining respectful, even if the opposing side of the case is antagonistic or staring with the intent to incite. The PI must never talk to a witness in the courthouse, or the result may be that opposing side can call the PI to the stand and ask what the PI said to the witness.

Preparation for Courtroom Testimony

The private investigator must make sure that his or her final report has been submitted along with any evidence, pictures, and signed statements. The PI should be very familiar with the case and the report, and he/she should review all of the documents before being called to testify.

Prior to trial, the PI should meet with the attorney who is the client and be prepped on possible questions that can be posed by the opposing counsel. The attorney client and PI should discuss strategies regarding possible questions asked and discuss what questions the attorney client will ask of the PI while he/she is on the stand. Additionally, the investigator and the attorney client should go over all evidence, pictures, and statements, to make sure these can be adequately presented in court.

Investigator Behavior during Testimony

When testifying on the stand in court, the private investigator must remain calm and not become excited over something said by the opposing attorney or by a command from the judge. The testimony from the PI should be clear and detailed, without the use of legalistic, complicated jargon or acronyms. Common phrases and language must be the norm when testifying. The PI must answer the question posed to him/her and not relinquish more information than what is asked for. All testimony from the PI must be presented as unbiased and factual. During testimony, the PI must not give the impression of being combative, even if provoked by the opposing attorney. The tone used by the PI should be calm, with an unfaltering voice and even physical manner.

Testimony Impeachment

On certain occasions in the courtroom, the private investigator will be called upon to challenge the validity of a witness's testimony. Obtaining a signed statement from a witness before the trial is always an investigative priority. If the witness has been influenced by bribes or other means and changes an accounting of the incident/accident while offering testimony on the stand, the investigator can produce the signed statement that might contradict what the witness is stating on the stand. The signed statement would impeach the testimony of the witness because he or she signed the statement prior to the trial.

The PI can also impeach a witness's testimony if factual documents are produced that show that the witness is a convicted felon or a chronic, illegal drug user. Other methods of testimony impeachment would be to show that the witness is biased because he/she is closely related to those involved in the trial, or the PI can demonstrate that the witness is biased because he/she has a vested interest in the case. The witness might also be biased because of a prejudice towards the investigator's client, but this must be proven with evidence, such as video or audio of the witness demonstrating prejudice.

Witness Preparation

When a trial is scheduled, and a witness is scheduled to testify, it is always a good idea for the PI to contact the witness and prep with him/her before trial. The witness should not be coached as to what to say on the stand, but the private investigator should have an idea of what the witness will say on the stand and relate the information to the attorney client. If a signed statement was previously taken from the witness, then the PI should show the witness the signed statement in order to refresh his or her memory, keeping the witness on track with the information in the signed statement. Sometimes a mock interrogation may take place where the PI asks the witness questions in a hostile manner, as an

opposing attorney might ask. This prepares the witness for what could happen while he/she is on the stand.

If the witness is scheduled to testify about documents that he or she is bringing to court, then those documents should be reviewed and evaluated with the PI, so there are no surprises to the attorney client when the witness testifies.

Sometimes the witness might have to testify to something that is embarrassing or controversial. It will be incumbent on the PI to convince the witness that his or her testimony is for the good of the case and that the witness must relate the information that is important to the case.

Preparation of Witness Types

There are a few witness *types*—personalities that should be identified and known before trial. A witness must be profiled and put into a category in order for the attorney client to know what he/she is dealing with when it comes time to put the witness up on the stand. When the witness is profiled, the private investigator will know how to deal with the witness and control the witness's emotions and reactions during preparation. A witness who is well prepared will be more emotionally even on the stand, without any unexpected outbursts or other strong feelings that will negatively influence the jury.

The following describes the six most common types of witness:

- The *know-it-all witness*: one with an intractable personality
- The *know-nothing witness*: one who claims to know just a few facts
- The *scared witness*: one who is apprehensive about taking the stand
- The *chatterbox witness*: one who offers too much information, won't stop talking
- The *minor witness*: children who are terrified of testifying and are easily intimidated
- The *expert witness*: a specialist in a certain field called to testify about findings or an evaluation

The Know-it-All Witness: This type of person will want to impress everyone with how smart he/she is and will insist on talking, even if the preferred testimony does not warrant it. The know-it-all witness will also insist that things were as he/she saw them. For example, she might insist a car was red, even though a picture of the car and the police report both state that the car was blue. This ilk of witness might be detrimental to the client's case if he/she were to irritate the jury or judge. The know-it-all witness should be used only if he/she has essential information for the case.

The Know-Nothing Witness: The Know-Nothing Witness might only know a few facts about the case and might not be worth putting on the stand. This type of witness might interject erroneous notions where hard facts contradict what he/she is saying. Straight, direct questions should be placed to this type of witness, and caution should be used in letting this type of witness ramble on with false information that could hurt the case.

The Scared Witness: Many people become frightened just at the thought of having to testify in court. A witness that acts terrified on the stand, so much so that he or she might stutter and not complete sentences, is a liability to the client's case. The scared witness must be questioned before the trial, and witness preparation is essential. A mock questioning period should take place to familiarize the scared witness with what possible questions or attitudes will be asked in court. After the PI assures the witness that he/she will be on the stand for a finite period of time and will not to be intimidated by the opposing counsel, the witness should then go to court soon after preparation.

The Chatterbox Witness: This type of person has a hard time keeping silent. The chatterbox witness will often keep talking long after the question has been answered. The jury and judge might get bored, irritated, or negatively enlightened if the chatterbox witness is permitted to continue talking past the simple answer to the question. The PI should inform the chatterbox witness that he or she should only answer the question and not go off on tangents about other subjects or drone on about the same thing already expressed. Sometimes, the attorney might have to cut the chatterbox orations short by cutting in and saying that he or she has answered the question and that will be all.

The Minor Witness: A child or young witness must be gently questioned and cajoled in preparation for court testimony. The minor witness is usually a school-age person who will be apprehensive about both taking the stand and testifying in court. The minor witness should be told that no one is going to yell or hurt him/her in court and that the judge is a very nice person who will make sure no one is allowed to be a bully. Elemental instructions should be given to the minor witness to just answer the questions truthfully and simply.

The Expert Witness: The attorneys involved in a trial will often call upon expert witnesses to bolster their cases. Medical expert witnesses are called to testify about medical records and conditions. Automobile expert witnesses are often on the stand giving their opinions on why a car's system failed contributing to an accident. An expert witness can be anyone who is certified in a certain field that reviews a document, person, or item that needs expert explanation given to a judge or jury. Expert witnesses should be prepped before a trial and listened to regarding what their determination of the evidence is. The client attorney will need to know what the expert witness will state before the trial.

Lay Witness and Expert Witness Testimony

While on the witness stand, both lay witnesses and expert witnesses can express opinions in court. However, the *lay witness* may only comment on those things that are of common sense or plain logic, such as hair color, height, and weight of a person or that a car was going too fast on the street when the car's engine roar was heard.

An *expert witness* may express opinions on matters of which he or she is considered an expert due to special training and education received. An expert witness might be a doctor who testifies on medical issues, or an expert witness might be a certified auto mechanic who has the credibility and expertise to testify on a vehicle in court.

Depositions

A deposition is usually held in a lawyer's office, but depositions can also take place in a courthouse or even a private home. A deposition has a stenographer present and sometimes a video camera recording the proceeding. Before a deposition, law offices, acting for the parties involved in the case, sometimes exchange interrogatories, which lay out some questions that have been summarily answered.

The many purposes for witness preparation before a deposition prepare the attorney client for what the witness will do and say at a deposition. The preparation before the deposition is also useful for knowing if the witness will be hostile to certain questions, what the witness's demeanor will be when asked volatile questions, and/or what the witness will bring with him/her in the form of documents.

Witnesses should be told that they have a right to refuse to answer a question and that if they do not understand a question, they have the right to say that they do not understand the question. During

preparation, the witness should be informed that they should not answer any question they do not fully understand.

Speculation at Deposition

During preparation of a witness before deposition, the witness should be informed that it is acceptable to give a judgment or an opinion concerning the facts. Sometimes a witness is hesitant to offer an opinion because he or she is not sure of the information. However, if asked, the witness can give his or her ideas on a subject he/she is knowledgeable about.

Adverse or Incomplete Deposition

If the testimony during a deposition was adverse or incomplete, the witness must be approached before trial and asked why the testimony offered during deposition was faulty. During this witness preparation, the gaps in the witness's testimony can be ascertained and later be explained to the opposing council while the witness is on the stand. This is better than having the witness try to cover up misstatements because a jury will be unforgiving if they think the witness is not telling the truth.

Types of Evidence

Hearsay Evidence

A witness is usually discounted in court if all he/she has to offer is hearsay evidence. If the witness did not actually observe an occurrence or was not in the vicinity to experience any part of an occurrence, then the witness has nothing to offer but hearsay evidence. When someone relates what he/she heard someone else say that is considered *hearsay* and may not hold much weight in court. Only the person who witnessed an event can be considered an actual witness to offer direct testimony.

There are some exceptions in court regarding the acceptance of hearsay:

- A dying declaration that is heard by someone and then repeated for the court might be considered as evidence

- Spontaneous declarations, such as "I didn't mean to kill her!"

- Former testimony, such as "The defendant did not stab the victim."

- Past recollection recorded on audio

- Business records, such as accounting pages that can be testified to

- Confessions and admissions, such as if a witness heard a person say, "I shot him because he had a knife."

Admissible Evidence

Three types of evidence are admissible in court: Testimony of a Witness, Documentary Evidence, and Physical Evidence.

Testimony of a Witness: If a person has witnessed or heard anything relating to case, then he or she may testify in court regarding any recollections. A witness can testify on anything that he/she has absorbed through his five senses.

Documentary Evidence: This form of evidence is easy to produce in court because it is physical. Documents, audio recordings, pictures, and accounting ledgers are examples of hard, physical type evidence, which can be entered into evidence during a case.

Physical Evidence: Any solid material or object that can be cataloged is physical evidence. Fingerprints on objects, weapons, blood, vomit, skin cells, or anything else that is in the physical world can be considered as physical evidence.

Spontaneous Declaration

A witness that hears a spontaneous declaration may testify in court about what he or she heard. This would be because the circumstances that surrounded the spontaneous declaration were of some urgency and a reaction to those circumstances could not have been rehearsed. When a shocking event has taken place, a person usually expresses things in a spontaneous manner, and this evocation may be used in court.

Dying Declaration

A dying declaration is made by a person who is dying and has made a statement before death. The circumstances of dying declaration make it possible to accept the dying person's statements into evidence. For example, the dying person can identify the perpetrator of his or her death. In order to have the dying declaration accepted into evidence, the person who made the declaration has to have died and, while dying, made the statement with a clear mind.

Past Recollection Recorded

A past recollection recorded is a reference to notes taken in order for the person to remember what had been done or said. This type of evidence cannot usually be submitted by itself; it must be accompanied by a witness who was the author of the notes. A common example of past recollection recorded is an investigator's notes read at trial. The notes were written when the memory of the occurrence was fresh in the investigator's memory. The opposing counsel must approve of the notes for them to be accepted into evidence at trial.

Former Testimony

A transcript or document produced at a trial or hearing that was previously given during a legal proceeding may be accepted as evidence at the present legal proceeding. The only time this exception is granted is when the witness is unavailable for the current legal proceeding.

Admissibility of Evidence

Confessions and Admissions

Confessions are usually documented in signed statements or video tapes; however, if an investigator received a confession spontaneously, then the investigator can make written notes and retain these notes for trial. The legal theory is that an innocent person would not admit or confess a crime unless he/she perpetrated the crime. Therefore, the notes that the investigator had taken at the time might hold up in court and be accepted as evidence. An investigator does not have to read someone a Miranda Warning; that is only for sworn law enforcement officials.

Business Records

Business records are kept by someone who works in an establishment that retains records in order to operate the business efficiently. These business records can be financial ledgers, attendance records, job

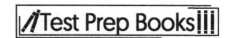

performance records, or inventory records. During trial, a qualified witness—most likely an employee of the business—will testify that the business records at trial were produced at the business by the witness or authored by others in the business.

Judicial Notice

The court can accept certain facts without proof at trial; however, any proof can be insisted upon by the parties. The trial can proceed with all parties accepting that judicial notices for certain precepts are understood to be true without question during the proceedings.

Admissibility of Character Evidence

Standard guidelines set by federal law prohibit assumptions to be made regarding crimes and accusing someone of that crime by his or her character. This is known as *Federal Rules of Evidence 404*, which states that a person cannot be accused of a crime just because he/she has the character to commit the crime. There are exceptions to the rule:

- A prosecutor may submit issues of peacefulness in a homicide case, where the victim was known to be peaceful but had made the initial aggressive action.

- Rule 608 enables the district attorney to prove the truthfulness or untruthfulness in court.

- Another exception is when the evidence of the trait of the person is congruent with the crime committed.

Legal Concepts

Presumption of Innocence

Presumption of innocence holds true in all criminal court proceedings. The prosecution has the *burden of proof* to prove, without a shadow of a doubt, that the accused is guilty of a crime. The defense does not have to prove that the client is innocent because innocence is presumed. However, the defense does have to prove that the client is innocent of the specific charges against the accused and that any evidence produced at trial does not have any connection to the accused. Even though the client is presumed innocent, a judge may order a remand for jail until the disposition of the court case is complete or if he/she feels the defendant is a flight risk or a threat to society.

Sixth Amendment

Bias and prejudice are not factors in a trial because then the accused would not be judged fairly. The United States Constitution ensures that a trial must be fair and impartial. The Sixth Amendment ensures that the defendant receives proper counseling during all stages of the criminal justice process, from pre-trial custody to appellation of the sentence.

The Sixth Amendment guarantees the following:

In all criminal prosecutions, the accused shall enjoy the right to a speedy and public trial, by an impartial jury of the State and district wherein the crime shall have been committed, which district shall have been previously ascertained by law, and to be informed of the nature and cause of the accusation; to be confronted with the witnesses against him; to have compulsory process for obtaining witnesses in his favor, and to have the Assistance of Counsel for his defense.

Eighth Amendment

After an accused person has been arrested and considered a defendant in the legal system, the Eighth Amendment guarantees that "excessive bail shall not be required." A defendant has a right to post money to ensure his/her appearance at the time of trial. If the defendant fails to appear at the trial, he/she has to bear the cost of the bail. The Eighth Amendment does not guarantee bail to all defendants.

If bail is granted, then it must not be excessive. A judge may deny bail in a homicide case or if the accused is a known felon who will most likely not appear for trial. The Amendment proclaims that excessive fines shall not be imposed, "nor cruel and unusual punishments inflicted." The Eighth Amendment protects incarcerated person from being abused in correctional facilities.

Fourteenth Amendment

Section 1 of the Fourteenth Amendment proclaims the following:

All persons born or naturalized in the United States and subject to the jurisdiction thereof, are citizens of the United States and of the State wherein they reside. No State shall make or enforce any law which shall abridge the privileges or immunities of citizens of the United States; nor shall any State deprive any person of life, liberty, or property, without due process of law; nor deny to any person within its jurisdiction the equal protection of the laws.

The Fourteenth Amendment is a United States federal edict, which supersedes state laws. This amendment commands that no state of the United States has legal power over United States federal laws, especially when it concerns *civil rights*. The Fourteenth Amendment also proclaims that any state in the United States must go through a due process of law to legally "deprive any person of life, liberty, or property" and that all persons have equal protections under state laws.

Practice Questions

1. What is a private investigator's first priority?
   a. The interpretation of the laws inherent in the case
   b. The welfare and satisfaction of the client
   c. The use of proper investigation techniques to make the case valid
   d. That all final reports conform to a standard

2. What is the difference between an *incident* and an *accident*?
   a. They are the same; it just depends on whether the victim is a man or a woman.
   b. If it was an incident, then it was not a crime, and police are not involved.
   c. An incident is intentional; an accident is unintentional.
   d. Police are concerned with both, but less priority is given to accidents.

3. Which type of report best describes a surveillance report?
   a. A daily report
   b. A chronological report
   c. A security survey report
   d. A narrative report

4. Which section of a final report should be considered the most important?
   a. The conclusion
   b. The header
   c. The opinion
   d. The executive summary

5. What is one reason why witness preparation before a trial is important?
   a. The investigator will know what the witness will say and inform the lawyer.
   b. The witness will need to know what to say and will need to rehearse his or her testimony.
   c. The witness will need money for lunch and new clothes to wear for court.
   d. During the trial, the judge will ask the investigator if the witness will cooperate.

6. Entrapment is a term used when law enforcement _____.
   a. Equips SWAT officers to trap criminals in a house during a drug arrest and then convinces the perpetrators to cooperate and become informants.
   b. Compels a person to act illegally when the person would not ordinarily act illegally.
   c. Lays out spike strips across a road to stop a speeding car.
   d. Catches a criminal during a crime and then compels the criminal to confess.

7. What does the term "Modus Operandi" refer to?
   a. The type of gear mode operated by a driver just before a car accident
   b. The type of surgery performed by an expert witness who is a doctor
   c. The method of operation or the way a person or group does something
   d. A description of the way a person walks in a video during a civil trial

8. What are the best terms to adhere to when taking investigation notes?
    a. Who, What, Where, When, Why, and How
    b. Investigate, Assimilate, Integrate, Promulgate, and Conclude
    c. Search, Find, Report, Opinion, Invoice, and Discuss
    d. Inform, Compile, Coordinate, Complete, and Report

9. Which description best represents the meaning of *Bright Line Standard*?
    a. The point during an investigation when the facts are agreed upon
    b. The line that an intoxicated person walks during a DWI police check point
    c. When a single factor determines the criteria in a legal decision or an arrest
    d. The standard reached when an investigator satisfactorily completes a court case

10. What are the three types of evidence admissible in court?
    a. Hearsay Testimony, Contrary Evidence, and Television Evidence
    b. Testimony of a Witness, Documentary Evidence, and Physical Evidence
    c. Canine Identification, Justice of the Peace Orations, and Bible Passages
    d. Misfeasance, Malfeasance, and Nonfeasance

11. Which sentence best describes *indictment* and *arraignment*?
    a. Indictment and arraignment are insurance terms used to describe an accident claim and a collision payment.
    b. This is when a person is falsely arrested and then mistakenly sent to jail.
    c. A determination of charge(s) is made in the indictment phase, and then the charges are read to the accused in the arraignment phase of a criminal court process.
    d. An indictment is when one spouse accuses the other spouse of infidelity and, arraignment is when the spouse files for divorce.

12. How should a private investigator dress for court?
    a. In a sport jacket with an open collar and nice slacks to convey an everyday appearance
    b. Any clothes, because the jury cares about testimony, not appearances.
    c. A suit and tie, because it shows a professional manner
    d. An open collar shirt and jeans, so that the jury doesn't consider the PI too elitist

13. What would be the best way for a private investigator to impeach a witness?
    a. The investigator buys the witness a fruit basket to make the witness cooperate because he/she has received a nice gift.
    b. In court, the investigator raises his hand to speak. Then, the investigator can tell the judge that the witness is not a believable person because the witness's ex-wife said he is a liar and owes child support.
    c. The investigator produces a signed statement that contains information contradictory to what the witness is presently claiming.
    d. The investigator testifies that the witness is a liar in order to provoke the witness, hoping that the witness yells at him/her, thus leading the jury to think the witness is not telling the truth.

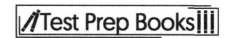

14. What is the best feature of the private investigation report for a private investigator?
a. The opinion and recommendations section, where the PI can include a section on how to continue an investigation
b. The marketing potential of a great report, so the client will freely give a good reference to friends and will want to use the PI again
c. A report conclusion, which means that the PI can submit an invoice and the client won't mind paying
d. The invoice, because without an invoice, the PI might not get paid

15. When can former testimony be accepted as evidence?
a. It can only be accepted when the former testimony is in the form of a video tape to verify what the witness said and under what conditions the witness gave the testimony.
b. The former testimony can be evidence if a member of the witness's family verifies the witness and swears that the witness's former testimony was true.
c. The court can accept former testimony that was given in a former legal proceeding, if the witness is not available for court.
d. Former testimony is not legal evidence because the witness is not present to swear to the testimony at court.

Answer Explanations

1. B: The welfare and satisfaction of the client. The private investigator must work to the client's benefit. All laws should be observed when performing investigations; otherwise, the investigator does the client a disservice and opens the PI business to negative civil litigation.

2. C: An incident is intentional; an accident is unintentional. Many people confuse the two different terms. The word *incident* is commonly used when the word *accident* would be technically correct.

3. B: A chronological report. The surveillance report is laid out to conform to the flow of time within a few hours. The report progresses as the observations of the investigator are recorded in concert with forward real time.

4. D: The executive summary. A professional client with many cases to review will appreciate the succinctness of a well-written executive summary. The client will know how to deal with his or her case in less time, due to the detailed, yet brief, executive summary at the start of a report.

5. A: The investigator will know what the witness will say and inform the lawyer. The private investigator is a transmitter of facts. The information that the investigator has received from the witness must be submitted to the lawyer on the case.

6. B: To compel a person to act illegally when the person would not ordinarily act illegally. In common parlance, entrapment is to *frame* or *set up* a person in order for law enforcement to obtain a prosecution and/or conviction.

7. C: The method of operation or the way a person or group does something. Modus operandi (MO) is a Latin term for method of operation. An MO is a useful tool for tracking and apprehending repeat offenders.

8. A: Who, What, Where, When, Why, and How. All investigations must follow these six venues of description, in order to relate the entire context of an occurrence.

9. C: When a single factor determines the criteria in a legal decision or an arrest. Some legal cases hinge on many factors, but some cases have just one factor that is the reason for the legal issue.

10. B: Testimony of a witness, documentary evidence, and physical evidence. A very basic understanding of the law will demonstrate that these three basic requirements are the foundations for evidence at a trial.

11. C: A determination of charge(s) is made in the indictment phase, and then, the charges are read to the accused in the arraignment phase of a criminal court process. Grand juries, often convened in secret and working with the district attorney, are tasked with determining if there should be a charge and what the charge should be. Then, an arraignment court hearing is held to voice charges to the accused.

12. C: A suit and tie, because it shows a professional manner. The private investigator should be in court for professional reasons only. Business attire, such as a suit and tie, is expected by the judge and jury, and it lends credibility to the private investigator's image.

13. C: The investigator produces a signed statement that contains information that is contradictory to what the witness is presently claiming. If the investigator was savvy enough to obtain the witness's statement on a signed paper, audio tape, or video tape with audio, it would be difficult for the witness to be convincing or change what he had originally told the investigator.

14. B: The marketing potential of a great report, so the client will freely give a good reference to friends and will want to use the PI again. A good report is like advertising. The better the report, the greater advertising potential.

15. C: The court can accept former testimony that was given in a former legal proceeding if the witness is not available for court. An example of former testimony would be if a process server who was served a summons passed away. The affidavit of service submitted at a previous hearing could be submitted into evidence at a subsequent court hearing, after the process server's death.

Case Management & Strategy

Case Management

Attorney Misconduct

Attorneys are governed by rules of professionalism set forth by the guidelines of the state they are licensed in. Attorneys are admitted to the *bar*; an official association that governs the conduct and adherence to official rules for attorneys in that state. Attorneys must maintain themselves in a professional decorum consistent with those rules that govern their licensing. The American Bar Association has a set of published guidelines which are universal for all states. Federal court also has superseding guidelines of ethics to follow when practicing on the federal level. Below is a list of some of the major ethical violations that govern attorneys but is not an all-inclusive list as the details can vary slightly from state to state:

- An attorney is obligated to maintain confidentiality of information received from their client.
- An attorney must keep safe the funds, documents, and other tangibles of their clients.
- The attorney should not put their own interests over their clients.
- The attorney must report any conflicts of interest in representation.
- The attorney must not engage in deceitful practices.
- The attorney must not try to unduly influence judges or court personnel.

Ethics and professionalism guidelines will vary from state to state but in essence, attorneys are governed by a set of professional standards and violating those standards can result in a loss of the license to practice law.

Ethical Issues

Private investigators during the course of their investigations are exposed to confidential information. They can also uncover new evidence which can bolster or weaken a case. It is among these reasons and others that investigators may face challenges to their integrity. Similar to attorneys, private investigators are also governed by their respective state's licensing law in regard to professionalism and ethical behavior. Some of the ethical dilemmas an investigator may face could be:

- The temptation to violate an individual's right to privacy in order to obtain evidence the investigator may need to prove a case.

- The temptation to disclose confidential information in order to obtain more information.

- The temptation to use coercion, lies, threats, or overt dishonestly to get information to help support the private investigator's case.

- The temptation to suppress evidence uncovered which may be contrary to the investigator's theory in the course of the investigation.

- The temptation to get personally involved in a case to the extent that it affects a private investigator's reasonable judgment.

Workplace Conflicts

In today's workplace, litigation abounds with employers and employees facing allegations of sexually inappropriate behavior, religious and gender discrimination, and compensation disputes, along with many other types of legally recognized workplace conflicts. Investigators may find themselves exposed to workplace conflicts and should be aware of best practices of how to respond.

- If the investigator is exposed to a discrimination complaint during the course of their investigation, they should report it to management of the organization for further investigation.

- If the allegation is of a criminal nature, then the investigator should advise the subject to file a police complaint. The investigator can only file a criminal complaint on behalf of the subject if the investigator themselves witnessed the criminal act.

- The investigator should be aware of federal, state, and local regulations and guidelines pertaining to the type of discrimination or complaint they are investigating.

- The investigator should be aware that many of these complaints, even if appearing frivolous, can progress to a civil or in some cases criminal court which is why it is important to document the facts of the complainant.

The private investigator may be confronted during the course of their investigation with employee sabotage, harassment, or fraud. Examples could be work slowdowns, the omission of critical information for managers or department heads to make informed decisions, erasing data, sharing sensitive data with competitors or vendors, etc. The private investigator should be cognizant of these types of activities and should identify and report on conflicts they discover during the course of the investigation. Based upon the conflict, the investigator may be called upon to perform the role of mediator.

Conflict Resolution

During the course of an investigation the investigator may come across a broad range of conflicts between the various parties involved in the investigation. The investigator may need to assist in conflict resolution in order to permit the investigation to be fruitful. A professional investigator must consider:

- The investigator must determine if the investigation would benefit from conflict resolution.

- How much authority does the investigator have between conflicting parties?

- The investigator must determine how many stakeholders are involved in the conflict.

- How critical is the conflict to the investigation? Will stakeholder's behaviors interfere with the investigation?

- The investigator must coordinate with the authorized or acknowledged negotiator or stakeholder for each party involved.

In some cases where the conflict has been longstanding or deep, an independent arbitrator with more experience in working through conflicts should be considered.

Conflict resolution is trying to provide a favorable outcome for all parties involved prior to expending a large amount of time and resources with a civil court proceeding. Conflict resolution generally involves a compromise on all sides. All parties are in agreement to each other's terms. A third impartial/non-involved party can be successful in conflict resolution because they can open up a better dialogue.

Private investigators should be aware of the process of arbitration and mediation as the knowledge of alternate forms of conflict resolution can useful to have.

Attorney-Client Fee Conflict Resolution

Some attorneys don't always disclose their fee schedule. A client can be charged for everything from sending an email, responding to a telephone call, or the response to a question. Most attorneys will bill in 15-minute increments even if the task didn't take 15 minutes. Some attorneys may continue to charge a client without discussing a cap beforehand which can end up costing more than the value of the case the attorney is pursuing for the client. To avoid being the subject of lawsuits, some attorneys have written arbitration and conflict resolution mechanisms in the actual attorney/client contracts. The designed intent is to work towards resolution on issues of cost and performance in order to avoid expensive litigation.

Alternative Dispute Resolution or "ADR"

Simply put, Alternative Dispute Resolution (ADR) is the mechanism employed to try to settle disputes by any means outside of the courtroom. This can involve any argument or suit that can be heard on the federal, state, and local level. In summary, it consists of the evaluation of the argument by both parties through negotiation, conciliation, mediation, and in some cases arbitration which can be binding or non-binding. Its goal is to provide reasonable relief for both parties while not burdening the civil justice system. It is valued by opposing sides as well as the court of jurisdiction because it will generally move quicker and cost less than traditional lawsuits. In addition, the arbitrator is usually highly skilled and can also produce a better outcome than the traditional civil court might otherwise render.

The types of cases that can benefit from ADR are:

- Employee benefit and tenure related issues
- Divorce proceedings
- Sexual harassment and discrimination related claims
- Wage and compensation issues

Each case within the ADR process falls under the supervision of an administrator. It is the role of the administrator to supervise the ADR budget, assign qualified resources to the case, liaison with the court, and provide transparency to the functions and findings of the ADR. This also includes evaluation of resource allocation, the outcome of services, and modification to program services where appropriate.

The federally funded Alternative Dispute Resolution service appoints a special counsel who reports directly to the United States Attorney General. The appointed Special Counsel represents the agency in external matters and serves as the Dispute Resolution Specialist for the United States Department of Justice.

Federal Mediation and Conciliation Service

In 1947 the federal government created an agency known as the "Federal Mediation and Conciliation Service" with a role to preserve and promote peace and cooperation between labor and management. The Federal Mediation and Conciliation Service provides mediation and conflict resolution services to industry, government agencies, and communities throughout the nation with the purpose of alleviating

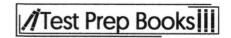

the workload of the federal court system. Similar to the ADR they provide an alternative to lengthy and costly trials and offer skilled negotiators in conflict resolution.

The Administrative Dispute Resolution Act of 1996

Administrative Dispute Resolution Act originates in Chapter 5; title 5 of the United States Code offers federal agency heads classified under section 573 the resolution power within their respective agencies to settle disputes outside of federal courts. The Administrative Resolution Act of 1996 reinforces and, in some cases, supersedes certain aspects of the act governing the role of the Federal Mediation and Conciliation Service. Specifically, it reinforces that only employees trained and qualified in conformance with section 573 of title 5, United States Code may act as neutrals and that they need to be adequately trained and can aid both parties in matters related to administrative programs. This process is not appropriate for every dispute and arbitrators may deny the process if they feel it doesn't fall within the intended scope, is part of a larger issue which might involve a precedent, or policy change or an issue that may require greater transparency.

Arbitration

Arbitration is the settling of a dispute between two parties by a third neutral party. Arbitration can be binding which means its findings must be followed by both parties or non-binding, which means if one or both of the parties are not pleased with the findings, they can seek other remedy.

Arbitration on the federal level can be considered when:

- The persons involved have full negotiating authority on behalf of their argument.
- The range of possible outcomes must be finite and specified.
- The willingness to enter into arbitration is not offered to obtain a benefit.
- If the outcome is expected to be binding, the arbitrator should consult with the attorney general.

Arbitrator

To be appointed as an arbitrator in accordance with the Administrative Dispute Resolution Act of 1996 the arbitrator should meet the following criteria:

- The appointed arbitrator must be a person that is agreeable to both parties.

- The arbitrator must not have a conflict of interest in the case they are hearing. If they do, they must state it to both parties who must agree to proceed despite the conflict of interest.

- The arbitrator can be replaced by either side at any time upon request.

- The arbitrator should have conflict resolution experience and come from a specialized agency that deals in negotiations.

Arbitrator Authority

The arbitrator has authority to govern the proceeding in accordance with the provisions of the Administrative Dispute Resolution Act of 1996. The arbitrator regulates the time frame for resolution, sets hearing dates and times, makes formal notifications, and assists both sides with solution strategy geared towards final resolution.

Arbitration Schedule of Proceedings

The Administrative Dispute Resolution Act outlines the schedule of proceedings towards final settlement:

- When setting a hearing, the arbitrator must provide at least 5 days' notice to the involved parties.

- The arbitrator should take the role of educator and brief the parties on the process and expectations of the proceedings along with the rules that govern it explaining it in laypersons terms for ease of comprehension.

- The arbitrator should determine and cap reasonable costs and assign those costs as prudently as possible. For example, if one side came unprepared for the hearing, the arbitrator could assign the day's costs for both sides to the side that was unprepared.

- The arbitrator should allow for discovery, presentation of the evidence, witness presentation, and cross examination to consider all evidence. However, since this is not a court proceeding, the presentation and discussion can be informal and is not sworn testimony.

- The arbitrator can allow parties to attend via telephone or video if travel is too difficult and can allow recordings only if consented to by both parties. Generally, phones and recording devices are not permitted into federal courtrooms without permission from the court. The arbitrator should provide any technical assistance for the conflict resolution hearing.

- The arbitrator should be prudent with the ADR resources and proceed efficiently.

- The arbitrator should look to make an award within 30 days or sooner of the completion of the final hearing unless either side requests otherwise.

The goal of the ADR is to make both sides get a balance of benefit and compromise to the extent they can settle and avoid a costly and lengthy trial process.

Mediation

95% or more of civil cases never make it to a verdict and are settled out prior to trial or during trial. The federal court understanding this phenomenon attempts to conserve its resources and strongly encourages parties to enter into Administrative Dispute Resolution prior to proceeding directly to trial.

If entering into the process to avoid assigning the case to Federal District Court for trial, both parties will be obligated to participate in discovery and share documents that the other feels may be useful to support their argument. They will provide statements of facts and quantify or qualify the issues of dispute if available. The magistrate must have all documents and positions submitted at least 10 days prior to the conference so they can review and prepare for the settlement conference. Parties in attendance must have full negotiation/settlement authority as not to unduly waste the arbitrator's time and resources.

The arbitrator in the ADR, typically a federal district court magistrate, will serve as a referee, setting timeframes and guideline, and providing instructions within the rules that govern the process. The proceedings shall remain confidential, and if the case is scheduled for formal court proceedings and the

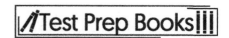

arbitration is implemented to avoid a federal court hearing, then the arbitrator cannot share facts of the arbitration with the judge scheduled for the formal hearing unless both parties consent to do so.

The arbitrator will not disclose informal discussions with either side to the opposing side unless given permission by the other party to do so. The arbitrator would be expected to meet with both sides together and then independently in order to nullify opposition to settlement. The settlement conference will either end in a reasonable settlement or will conclude without disposition and possibly proceed to other action.

Mediation in Franchise Law

Because of the abundance of franchise relationships, the court can order mediation for parties involved in franchise disputes under the Federal Rules of Civil Procedure law. The court in most cases will demand court ordered mediation in order to conserve court resources and expedite the resolution of the dispute. This is advantageous to franchise related parties because it is expedient in permitting them to resolve the issues and getting the parties back to their business relationship. In addition, with mediation's lower costs the money stays in the business coffers of the parties. The mediation is not binding, so if either party does not agree to settlement, they still have the opportunity to proceed to formal litigation.

Summary Jury/Bench Trial

A summary jury or bench trial process is similar to that of the formal court process but unlike the formal court process it is not binding. A jury or magistrate is presented with opening statements, evidence, arguments, and closing statements from each opposing party. After consideration the judge or jury must render their decision in a relatively short time frame of a day or less, but the decision is not binding. This process will also provide some insight to each party on how a formal process would proceed should it get to that stage.

Early Neutral Evaluation

If the dispute appears to be unavoidable for trial after dispute resolution fails, then Early Neutral Evaluation (ENE) commences. This process is basically a non-trial process to size the dispute up to ensure it fits within legal parameters to proceed. It is common for the EME to evaluate any last-ditch efforts at resolution. If the case looks like it is going to proceed, they will try to determine fact from fiction while placing a monetary estimate on the value of the dispute.

Conflict of Interest

A conflict of interest arises when an individual, who is supposed to be neutral or impartial, has a gain or a benefit that will be derived from an outcome they can help decide or are otherwise involved in. An example would be a juror in a hearing who is related to the defendant. Because of that close relationship, the juror has a conflict in that they are predisposed to not convict their own relative even if the evidence suggests otherwise. It is for that reason that court proceedings need to clear up any conflicts of interests affecting all parties involved in the legal process.

Attorneys, jurors, judges, and others are required to declare any conflicts of interest so they can recuse themselves. In certain instances, once the conflict is declared, the person with the conflict may still be able to participate but only after all parties are aware and comfortable with the conflict, understanding that it won't unduly influence them in the decision. The investigator should also make known to any parties involved in the court proceedings of any conflict of interest the investigator may have. The investigator may be recused from the investigation in order to eliminate any suspicion of impropriety.

Attorney-Client Conflict of Interest

The Sixth Amendment of the United States Constitution provides citizens the right to a speedy trial, a fair jury, and an attorney if requested which will be afforded if they cannot afford one. The Sixth Amendment delves further into legal protection and guarantees against an attorney conflict of interest. There can be several reasons why an attorney can have a conflict of interest. For instance, trying to represent both parties in a dispute, having a personal relationship with someone who is part of the current court process, or representing two separate clients with competing interests in the same case or a closely related case would represent conflicts of interest. In essence, it is something that the attorney will get personal gain from that may not make them as compelled to defend the client to their fullest extent based upon personal gain or benefit from a personal relationship.

Fiduciary Duty and Fiduciary Conflict of Interest

Fiduciary duty is a legal duty to manage financial transactions and accountability solely in another party's interest as opposed to their own or a third party's. People that are charged with these duties are known as *fiduciaries*. They are usually in positions of trust such as a controller in a larger corporation who oversees all financial transactions for the owner or the principal of the company. The person or persons charged with the fiduciary duty must exercise legally recognized business practices and cannot act in any way that puts their own financial gain or benefit over that of the owner or principal. If they have a conflict in their duties, they are required to report it so arrangements for oversight or transfer of those duties can be made with the principal's informed consent.

Confidential and Privileged Communication

Many types of communication are considered *privileged* and *confidential* which is a recognized court term to protect information from falling into opposing side's hands, which may unduly affect the outcome of a case. The client should also have an expectation of privacy in that they can tell things to their attorney to prepare for defense that they may not want a judge or jury to know. They are bound by confidentiality attorney-client privilege to keep the information confidential. There are certain instances however when confidential information can be shared at the appropriate times in the following circumstances:

- If the information is shared with the consent of the person or persons who provided it. An example would be if the client emailed the attorney confidential information and then later in the discovery process the client gave the attorney permission to introduce that email to the court.

- If the information is already made public, it has no provision of confidentiality. An example will be if a defendant in a criminal trial was arrested and during that arrest made a statement to the newspaper that they were guilty. That statement because it was offered of free will and was published may be introduced in court and is not protected by confidentiality restrictions.

- The information can be disclosed if the gravity of the information greatly outweighs the outcome of the current proceedings especially if it involves a public safety issue. An example would be if a client told his attorney that a bomb was hidden in the court room. In the interest of greater public safety, the attorney could disclose this information on a need-to-know basis to those having authority over the public safety issue.

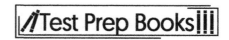

- Besides breaching confidentiality in the interest of public safety, the court has also ruled that confidentiality can be breached to prevent injustice.

- The importance of the confidential information is more important than the case it is involved in.

Rule of Privileged Communications

Some personal and professional relationships are considered privileged and can be protected from being introduced into court proceedings. Some examples are a clergy-penitent, attorney-client, and physician-patient relationship. In some states, the rules can extend to a psychotherapist or reporter. Personal conversations between a husband and wife can also be privileged. In order for the court to consider it privileged the communication must:

- Have taken place in a private setting with a reasonable expectation of privacy.
- It should not be told to a third party who would breach its confidentiality.
- The privilege can be waived if both parties agree.

Husband-Wife Privilege

As a general rule, private conversations between a husband and wife are protected by confidentiality. The only exceptions to pierce that confidentiality would be if the spouses were coconspirators in a crime, if the spouses are opposing each other in court, or if one of the spouses is charged with an offense against the other, their joint property, or their child. A husband or wife cannot be forced to testify against each other.

Attorney-Client Privilege

As a general rule all communications between a client and their attorney is considered confidential. This protection extends to both written and spoken word. Even if a client admits guilt to their attorney, the attorney must keep that confidential at the request of the client and advocate for the client's innocence. The only exception would be if both the attorney and client mutually agree to disclose the guilt to the court. This protection solely protects client-attorney communication and does not extend to clerks, paralegals, or those not admitted to the bar or identified as the attorney of record.

Accountant-Client Privilege

In general, while an accountant-client privilege is recognized in some state and federal actions, it is not applicable in a criminal proceeding. The *Internal Revenue Service Restructuring and Reform Act of 1998* provides protection between a client and their federally authorized tax preparer which can also be their accountant in non-criminal matters.

The accountant-client privilege protection falls into two categories: evidentiary and non-evidentiary. Evidentiary can be asserted favorably in a court of law. Non-evidentiary is when the protection cannot be asserted in a court of law or when it is deemed not applicable in response to a court order for disclosure. There are time limits associated with these protections based upon the date the legislation was enacted. Accountant-client privilege is not applicable prior to July 22, 1998, and tax specific information is not protected prior to October 22, 2004.

Physician-Patient Privilege

Physician-patient privilege is recognized at both the federal and state level. Under the federal *Health Insurance Portability and Accountability Act (HIPAA)*, protection is provided against disclosure of physician-patient information to third parties without the patient's consent. The premise behind this is so that the patient feels comfortable enough to speak freely with a doctor without fear of exposure of the information to a third party. This privilege is not recognized under Federal Rules of Evidence and, depending upon the individual state legislation, may or may not be admitted in court proceedings. This would depend upon applicability with other related privacy laws in conjunction with the circumstances. Some states however do recognize the privilege and will ban the disclosure in state court. The physician-patient privilege only applies to the patient's treating physician and does not extend to physicians in general.

Law Enforcement-Informant Privilege

In certain instances, the court will protect the right of a police informant to remain anonymous and protect their identity. Precedent was established in this regard in 1957, in the *Roviaro v. United States case*, 353 U.S. 53, 63-65 where the court ruled that the privilege of the informant permits the government to seal the identity of the informant. The obvious reasons are to maintain their safety and keep their identity covert so they can continue to provide law enforcement intelligence without fear of retaliation from those they report crimes on.

The court also stated that while the informant-law enforcement privilege is recognized by the court, it is not absolute and was a "matter of balance" and could be determined on a case-by-case basis. Some circumstances when the informant-law enforcement privilege does not have to be upheld is when the intelligence provided by the informant is cast in serious doubt or when testimony by the informant for important information related to a crime outweighs whatever confidential intelligence they intended to provide.

Priest-Penitent Privilege

Much like the physician-patient privilege, the intent of the priest-penitent privilege is to permit the penitent the comfort of practicing their faith without fear of impunity for things they may want to reveal to their respective church but not to the court or public. The definition of what legally constitutes a "priest" can vary from state to state so it is best for the investigator to research local laws to confirm that classification. In some cases, the privilege can extend to counseling not directly part of the sacrament of confession and in other states the obligation to report child abuse can supersede the priest-penitent privilege.

Reporter-Source Privilege

The reporter-source privilege is based on the First Amendment in which the government recognizes that without protection on disclosure to reporters under free speech then that source of information would be reluctant to provide important information to news reporters and journalists and therefore the reporter under most circumstances may keep the identity of the source confidential.

Like most of the privileges outlined there are exceptions and jurisdictional limitations to the reporter-source privilege as well. The federal courts in most cases uphold the reporter-source privilege, but if the judge feels the balance of the information the court needs from the reporter outweighs the need to keep the source confidential, the judge can issue a subpoena which will compel the reporter to either disclose the source of information or to force them to protect the identity in a legal challenge or face contempt of court. On the state level, this protection can vary.

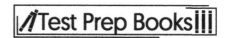

Developing and Implementing Strategies

Case Management System

Investigators generally manage multiple cases simultaneously. It is therefore important for investigators to identify and implement a case management system. In essence, a case management system is a system of record keeping and accountability for all the cases that may be active and archived. Some investigators rely on software programs to track their cases, and others may manage the process manually. The case management system should be designed to maintain a case file either in electronic or paper format and track the case with details of the origination of the case, pertinent background information, client contact information, evidence, records, photos, statements and any actions, updates to the file or note, and next dates of action or appearance.

It is also designed for file sharing with others that have clearance to view the file or update records. Case management is also useful in the event the case is transferred to another investigator. Case management software can also function for billing and receivable functions. In large firms a case manager is assigned to manage the cases, and in smaller organizations it may be a single investigator themselves that organizes their own case management.

Case management can refer to either the entire system of managing all the cases the investigative firm has, or it can refer to a case management plan for a single case. In either scenario, each case should have a primary lead person who manages and directs activities on that particular case as it moves along the investigative process.

Activities and Participants

When performing case management, whether the investigator is a one-person investigative firm or part of a multi-person organization, a case management system should be utilized to not only plot and track the case but also act as a central repository for all information and client contact relating to the case. The alternative of keeping the information in multiple places may not only challenge the credibility of the information when presented to a court of law, but it also increases the risk for information to be misplaced. All notes, interviews, activities, calls and all other pieces of information, even the simplest detail as it relates to the case, should be included in the case management file for future reference and file sharing.

Case Manager Duties

The case manager's role is to make sure the case file is established and in queue for subsequent action. The case manager should develop at the initiation stage of the case an action plan that is favorable to the outcome of the case. It is common for the case manager to speak to both the client and the lead investigator assigned to the case to identify projected costs, estimate timeframes of activity, forecast outcome expectations, and discuss anything else that may be of concern to all parties. The case manager oversees the case activity and should direct or redirect resources where needed to ensure expectations, as discussed with the clients, to come to fruition. The case manager should ensure that the case file is comprehensive with all related information and where the information originated. The case manager is responsible for documenting any changes in the status of the investigation.

The case manager shall maintain custody to ensure a record storage system in accordance with the legal timeframes of document retention as established by state and federal laws which stipulate timeframes on the preservation of document and business records.

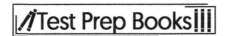

Case Management File

Identification System

Case files within a case management system should be assigned a *coding* for each case file for ease of identification and classification. The agency or investigator can establish a series of numbers, letters, or a combination that works best for their record keeping or use one of many computer filing software programs. The case identification system should include some reference to the date the case originated and the sequential number to identify when the case was received to track the volume of cases and identify the division, office, or investigator assigned.

An example for the first case of the year 2016 originating out of the investigative firm's New York office that was assigned to investigator John Doe can, as an illustration, be coded 01-15-16-NY-JD which would represent 01 (January), 15 (the 15th day of the month), 16 (The year 2016), NY (representing the New York office), and JD (representing investigator John Doe). This specific coding template is not an absolute template but some form of coding for reference should be used for the case tracking system.

Components

The case management file should include every document, recording, photo, and any other piece of evidence, report, or fact involved in the investigation. It should also include:

- The lead source or origination of where the case came from. Information should include who referred the case and who is the investigator's client

- It should contain a contract for services between the investigator and client.

- It should include billing information to include identifying the client point of contact and billing rates.

- It should include a schedule and summary of activity so others viewing the file can determine the action plan for the case and the current status.

- It should identify the case manager as well as the lead investigator assigned to the case.

- It should list all contact with the client with records of the summary of client contact via email, telephone, and in person with notes of what was discussed for future reference.

Computerized Case Management Systems

While manual case management systems may be preferred for lone investigators or small investigative firms due to the low volume and nominal cost of paper files, a *computerized tracking system* has multiple advantages over the manual process. Among those advantages are:

- The ability to manage a limitless volume of files due to the efficiency of the electronic system

- The ability to file share between multiple persons who may need access to the files

- The ability to store files without consuming office space

- The ability to locate files faster and easier than manual records

- If properly stored, the electronic files are not predisposed to being destroyed though fire, flood, or other natural disaster.

- The electronic file system can send reminders to the investigator for tasks to be completed in the form of a calendar and can actively assist the investigator as opposed to paper files which are static.

- The software program would permit managers to better track investigator productivity.

The only disadvantages associated with an electronic case management system are the costs associated with software purchases and the vulnerability to threats related to electronic files. For this purpose, an offsite backup for redundancy or cloud-based configuration is always recommended along with adequate security protections.

Formalized Case Management Procedures

Many state and local police agencies receive federal funds to support local law enforcement efforts. In exchange the federal government seeks to establish standardized reporting across the United States in an effort to properly classify and standardized crime reporting. As a result, the Federal Bureau of Investigation maintains the *Uniform Crime Reporting system,* or UCR, since it was established in 1930. The Uniform Crime Reporting is an effort towards mandating that all police agencies report crimes in standardized classifications with a universally recognized set of standard questions and other specific data requested so local investigators can report to the FBI annually on crime statistics in their region using the same methodology by all agencies.

Case Assignment

The assignment of a case can be predicated on multiple criterions and is generally assigned by the case manager after a review of the case's expected needs. The following are some of the criteria that are considered when assigning a case:

- A particular investigator's availability
- A particular investigator's current caseload
- A particular investigator's area of expertise or suitability as it applies to the investigation
- The geographic location of the investigator versus the geographic location of the investigation
- The priority or sensitivity of the case

Case Evaluation

In the initial interview with a potential client, the investigator should evaluate the client's motivation for seeking investigative services. In most instances, the need for investigative services is valid and has merit but in other cases the circumstances may be illicit or suspect. Therefore, the investigator should carefully screen the case to gain confidence that the potential client is of sound mind and body, that the intent of the investigation is lawful, and that the real purpose of the investigation is not masked by a fictitious story a client may offer to disguise the real intent.

In order for the investigator to proceed with the case, they should be comfortable that the scope of work is within their expertise, that the client has realistic expectations of the outcome, and that there is no ulterior motive for the client initiating the investigation.

Client Cost Discussions

The private investigator works for compensation to maintain their livelihood. As such, compensation should be discussed with the potential client as part of the initial screening of the case. Things to consider are:

- Providing clear estimates of expected time frames and costs for the investigation prior to beginning the work

- Having the client sign a contract that explains payment terms so they are informed and bound

- Discussing and negotiating costs based upon the means of the potential client and the volume of services requested. Generally, the more work the client will assign, the greater the discount that can be offered

- Discussing payment terms and types

- Accepting a retainer or fee in advance which the investigator can draw down on as services are performed

- Discussing with the client thresholds for replenishment of the retainer and what specific incidental costs they may want to approve

- In some cases, the investigator may encounter costs associated with surveillance such as tolls, parking, meals, lodging, etc. and these costs should also be discussed in advance with the client and written into the contract

Investigation Strategy Proposal

After the initial discussion with the potential client in person or via telephone, the investigator should summarize the conversation in the form of a proposal and send the proposal and contract to the potential client for review. It should include at a minimum:

- Any communication to the client should include the private investigators license number and any other special wording or information required, as governed by local private investigator licensing law

- Insurance information if required by local licensing law or if requested by the client

- Contact information for the investigator

- A summary of the discussion, expectations of outcome, timeframes, and anticipated costs of the investigation

- A copy of a contract for investigative services for the potential client to review

- A request for information from the potential client of what would be needed in order to initiate the investigation if they in fact consent to the service agreement

Competent Investigations

The success of the investigative case relies on the ability to properly assess the potential case requirements, the understanding of realistic outcomes, the availability of potential evidence, availability

of witnesses, and the access to facts leading to a conclusion of the investigation. If no information or lead sources are available or attainable, then the outcome expectations will be poor. As a general rule, the older the case is, the harder it will be to collect evidence with witnesses scarce or having poor recollection of details. The investigator should also only accept cases that are within their area of expertise, and if applicable, they should advise the client that they may have to bring in another professional to support the case such as a certified financial examiner or computer analyst to review financial transactions, etc.

Investigations don't always come to a conclusion. In some cases, they are mere fact-finding exercises and may terminate before a hypothesis is confirmed or supported. First and foremost, to ensure a competent investigation the investigator must be impartial, clear of any conflict of interest, and begin the investigation with objectivity. Once the investigator is deemed suitable based upon those criteria the following components make for a competent investigation.

- Comprehensive: The investigator should consider all possible evidence, witnesses, and other data that would permit all possible questions to be answered. In other words, the investigator should not take short cuts and should explore all possible avenues.

- Verified information: The investigator will come across multiple facts and evidence during the course of an investigation. The investigator must properly qualify each piece of information as to its authenticity and reliability. Some hard records like phone logs can easily be classified as verified and accurate. Other verbal statements for example from informants without a performance history or providing reliable information in the past can be classified as a general unverified statement. If the informant's information is corroborated by someone else the investigator can more likely identify that as verified as well. The investigator should make every attempt to verify or corroborate information.

- Relevance: The investigator should not convolute the investigation with irrelevant information obtained during the course of the investigation. The investigator should summarize statements only to include relative facts and statements.

- Current information: The investigator should have updated information as it pertains to the case. Outdated information can bring into question the competence of the investigator to maintain the case file in a timely manner.

Investigative Resources
The investigator must think comprehensively when deciding upon the investigative resources needed for a particular case. The following is a non-inclusive list of some of the investigative sources the investigator may seek:

- The internet: A powerful tool for gleaning facts on a subject's interests; from news reports, social media profiles, and other open internet sources.

- Interviews: Friends of the subject, neighbors, relatives, coworkers, employers, eyewitnesses, medical professionals, and anyone else that the investigator may think could supply some information to assist the investigation should be interviewed.

- Technology: The investigator should consider the use of audio/video recording after ensuring it meets with federal and state guidelines. Consider photography, GPS units, computer forensics, and any other technology which may assist the investigation.

- Surveillance: Consider surveillance to observe subjects and behaviors which may relate to the investigation.

- Documents: Determine which documents if any can support the investigation including marriage certificates, death certificates, licenses, phone records, financial reports, etc.

- Background information: Conducting an open-source background check on the subjects to be interviewed may prove useful to provide some insight into the person the investigator will interview.

- Evidence collection: Consider what evidence the investigator may need to successfully support the investigation. If the intent is to ultimately submit the evidence into civil or criminal court proceedings, then the investigator should follow universal crime scene collection guidelines and maintain a chain of custody on the evidence.

Investigation Plan

The investigative plan consists of four phases:

The Preparation Phase

The preparation phase should be used to permit the investigator to become oriented to the case in order to understand the dynamics involved. During this phase, the investigator should be identifying the possible needs for resources, specialists, man hours, equipment, and anything else that may be required for a successful investigative outcome. The investigator should also be clear on the type of investigation being conducted and the scope it will entail. The preparation phase should also involve communication with the client to confirm both that the investigator has the resources and experience for a successful investigative outcome and that the client understands and can afford the scope of services as envisioned by the investigator.

The Investigative Stage

In the next phase, the investigator should begin the actual investigation phase by collecting whatever evidence, statements, and documents are needed as determined in the preparation stage. In many cases the investigative stage may lead the investigator to other sources of information that were not known in the preparation stage, and the investigator should communicate that to the client to discuss additional resources and allocations that may be needed to pursue those new lead sources.

Notes are an important part of this stage. The notes of private investigators can be introduced in court as evidence. Notes should be taken during interviews to memorialize facts and statements that the interviewee is relating. The notes should be clear, concise, and to the point. The heading on the notes should include the date, subject of the interview, location, time of the interview, the case name or investigation it references, and any witnesses that may be present for the interview. The notes will used later for the investigator to draft a formal report.

The note-taking can be recorded in short statements from the interviewee. The notes should be made part of the case file as evidence or backup to a subsequent formal report the investigator may draft based upon those notes. Even if utilizing an audio or video recording device, notes should still accompany an interview as back up and to clarify statements that may not be audible on an audio recording.

The Analytical Phase

After conducting all the research and evidence collection, the investigator should analyze the findings to determine what inferences and conclusions the evidence suggests. The investigator should also sort out information that is verified from what is plausible but not corroborated and what was determined to be outright false or proven invalid based upon conflicting reports. After reviewing all the findings of the investigation, the investigator should be prepared to report to the client.

Inductive and Deductive Reasoning Phase

When arriving at conclusions, inductive and deductive reasoning can be utilized. Inductive reasoning involves examining several observations to arrive at a specific theory. An example of inductive reasoning would be if the investigator determined that a door was breached at a factory with burglary tools and then determined that all employees have keys. *Inductive reasoning* would conclude that the break-in was not done by an employee since all employees have keys and wouldn't need to break the door.

Deductive reasoning on the other hand takes a general statement and/or theory and then defines a conclusion. An example of deductive reasoning would be that all employees have a key to the factory therefore if John Doe is an employee of the factory then he must have a key.

Both reasoning techniques are slightly different, and it is very important to understand that both inductive and deductive reasoning can result in false outcomes. For example, in the inductive reasoning scenario just because employees have keys to the factory doesn't mean that they didn't avoid using their key to make it look like a burglary. Also, in the deductive reasoning example provided, just because all employees were issued keys doesn't mean that John Doe didn't lose his key, and an absolute assumption that he has the key is not valid until confirmed.

Debriefing

In the final stage at the conclusion of the investigation, the investigator will notify the client of the findings in a debriefing. The debriefing will provide the client an executive summary of the findings and will not generally contain the entire case file unless specifically requested to be reviewed by the client. The summary will purge any information obtained during the investigation that was not deemed useful or related and should only define facts or relevance which support the scope of the investigation.

All information between a client and investigator should remain confidential and should be classified as such. The investigator should also keep in mind that emails, documents, and notes can be subpoenaed by a court of law, and all records and communication should maintain a professional decorum. The debriefing can consist of a verbal summary supported by a written summary. This will permit the client to ask any additional questions, and then provide a confirmation of the findings for the client's use. The investigator may also discuss additional follow up or client referrals at this juncture.

Efficient Time Management

When conducting investigations, efficient time management is the key to an expedient work flow process which will result in client satisfaction, enhanced billing, increased profit, and the ability to manage a greater volume of cases. The following are some techniques to enable efficient time management:

- Organizing case files and documents: The easier it is to locate files and documents of the investigation the less time will be wasted searching for related documents. A good case management system will reduce wasted time that can be associated with disorganized case files.

- Focusing on the outcome of the investigation: Many times, investigators can get sidetracked in unrelated conversations or tasks that are not essential to the investigation outcome. Identify the investigative goals and stay focused on the outcome.

- Categorizing priorities: The investigator should sort tasks into categories such as those that are time critical, time sensitive, important, and routine. Properly identifying and classifying tasks will enable tasks to be managed in priority order.

- Handling tasks as they come in: If a simple task comes in that can be handled in a few moments, do it immediately instead of putting in on the desk with multiple other little tasks which can build up and have to be handled twice or more. This will avoid having the investigator touch the task again and expend more resources than necessary.

- Managing the work flow: Don't manage work as it comes in but rather plot the work flow based upon the priorities of what should be accomplished first. Failing to plan is a plan to fail.

- Delegating tasks properly: Some tasks are beneath the investigator's skill set and can be assigned to a lower salaried employee when available. Recognize what tasks should be assigned to the investigator and what tasks can be assigned to lower-level staff if available. This will permit the proper delegation of the task to the person with the appropriate skill level and allow the investigator to handle higher level tasks.

- Managing time effectively: Keep meetings and discussions on short but effective schedules to ensure they are efficient.

- Utilizing technology: Introduce technology where possible to eliminate or streamline tasks.

Scheduling Techniques

An efficient case management system is useful for scheduling tasks and duties. It can keep track of the investigator's appointments and help avoid scheduling conflicts. Since multiple investigations and interviews may be active simultaneously, it is best to consider conducting as many interviews as possible in a geographic area even if they relate to two different investigations. This will help reduce travel time for the investigator to go back to the same geographical area on another unrelated case. Where possible, schedule interviews over the phone in instances where the information the investigator seeks is routine to the investigation, and there is no value for the investigator to observe body language of the subject of the interview.

Recording Tasks and Costs

Transparent and open billing along with good record keeping will ensure smooth invoicing and subsequent payment. Before the case even begins, the client should have received from the investigator a contract with proposed fees and a written summary of the estimated scope of work and costs. Where possible, the investigator should consider a retainer or payment up front before the work begins. The investigator should also discuss with the client other related expenses for copies and clerical expenses, surveillance related expenses, lodging, or any other costs that may be involved in an investigation. Invoicing schedules should also be discussed prior to billing.

Electronic case management software can help keep track of billing related to the case, or the case manager can manually collect that data. Whatever method the firm chooses to record the time and resources associated with a case, it should follow a standardized system set up by the firm or investigator to ensure efficiency in billing. The investigator should also recognize that all time spent on the case even with indirect tasks such as the review of documents and copying should be assigned and billed to a client if related to their case.

Time and Expense Report

Accurate and complete business records related to time and expense need to be maintained for several reasons. Tax and business practice compliance is one of the main reasons along with client support, litigation defense, accounting, etc. The investigator should keep track of all time and expenses related to their work and as it relates to the respective case files. The investigator's expense report should be clear, concise, and reviewed and approved by a designated authority. The following list provides some examples of essential information needed on the expense report:

- The name of the investigator submitting the expense

- The date, location, and case reference the actual expense correlates with

- The investigative reason or basis for the expense

- The receipt for the expense should be attached or included in the file with the case number it references in the event it gets separated from the file.

- Mileage rates and meal expenses should follow generally accepted government standards by region which can be found at gsa.gov under "per diem" rates.

- If an electronic case management system is available, it can track these expenses.

- Expense thresholds should be discussed with management and the client beforehand for a clear understanding of what may be preapproved and what amount or type of expense requires further approval.

- A manager should sign off on all expense reimbursement requests for accountability.

Pre-Employment Investigations

Investigators are often called upon to perform pre-employment investigations for employers. The investigation should begin with a release for information signed by the job applicant for the specific background information requested. The search should be limited to the information described in the release. Typical areas of background check screening are:

- Drug use: Note that the subject must consent to a drug screen.

- Criminal history: Note that state laws vary on the types of inquiries that can be made in reference to criminal history for employment.

- Education verification

- Financial history: especially if the candidate is going to be working in positions of trust or handling money

- Medical history: only if consent is provided by the candidate

- Social media profiles: Investigators can review social media profiles for evidence of drug use, bias, or other employment concerns.

- Employment history: interviewing past employers or verifying past employment

- Personal reference interviews: interviewing social contacts for verification of the candidate's character

Inappropriate Employment Application Questions

Whether conducting employment interviews for a client or for the investigator's own firm, the following are considered inappropriate or unlawful questions based upon federal and state guidelines:

- Age
- Race
- Country of birth
- Gender
- Religion
- Marital status
- Sexual orientation
- Pregnancy status
- Disability related questions
- Military discharge papers
- In some states the criminal history of the candidate is off limits or protected by certain time period statutes or not permitted until after the candidate is considered approved for hiring. Check permissibility in the jurisdiction of operation.

It should be noted that while these questions are off limits, an interviewer can ask questions that are job or task related which may compel a candidate to reveal information related to one of these protections or the candidate can decline to disclose. An example would be asking a candidate being considered for a warehouse position if they have the ability to complete the related task of picking up boxes. If they have a disability which prevents them from doing so then they should either tell the interviewer they can't perform the task, or they may reveal that a certain disability prevents them from doing the task. This is acceptable because the investigator didn't ask about any disability but rather spoke about the job requirements and a condition of employment and whether the candidate could perform the task or not.

Computer Crime

With the advent of computer technology, computer crime has been increasing in frequency. Based upon the anonymity provided by the computer, the computer provides an excellent screen for criminal activity. In addition, jurisdictional boundaries also make internet crimes difficult to prosecute. A computer crime is committed when the computer is used either as the means of a crime, as an instrument in which the crime was committed, or when criminal evidence is stored within it. Listed below are the most common types of criminal activity involving a computer:

Computer Forgery

Because of their excellent copying abilities, computers are used for the illicit purpose to make fake government documents such as licenses, visas, checks, counterfeit money, and other false documents. Many original documents now incorporate the use of holograms and other safeguards making them more difficult to copy. There is technology available that can help identify fraudulent documents, and the investigator should be aware that counterfeit documents abound and can be undetectable from the original document depending upon the quality of the equipment and the material used in duplication.

Computer Fraud Manipulation

Computer fraud manipulation involves a sophisticated knowledge of the operating system along with some personal information of the target and involves changing or manipulating a computer record or transaction for illicit personal gain. Perpetrators could also manipulate invoices for fraudulent purposes or alter a program for illicit gain. An example would be entering someone's bank account electronically without their knowledge and having checks dispersed to a criminal operative. Common computer fraud manipulation manifests itself in billing schemes, inventory fraud, check tampering, payroll fraud, and other financial related activities.

Computer Unauthorized Access

An example of unauthorized computer access would be someone without permission breaching another person's computer externally which can take over their operating system. Work computers should be password protected with an auto lock. The password should be difficult to decode and should not be provided to others. External assaults through programs designed to take over an operating system are common. A computer should be updated with an adequate firewall, and computer operators should never open emails or attachments from unidentified persons. If an email appears suspicious from a known contact, then it is necessary to confirm the email is legitimate by using telephonic voice communications.

Computer Virus or Worms

Computer damage or file corruption can take place through a virus, a worm, or other infection software designed to corrupt files in the computer system. A strong firewall and enhanced computer security software should afford protection against most malware, viruses, and worms.

Computer Unauthorized Reproduction

The web provides a far-reaching range of opportunity for criminal enterprise including the duplication of copyrighted movies, songs, and other protected material. Major corporations along with the FBI are actively pursuing investigations into computerized copyright infringement due to the fact that the scale of activity is large enough that it significantly affects sales revenue.

Computer Crime Investigation

Procedures

It is not uncommon for the investigator to come across a possible evidence source which may involve a computer. The investigator must have the authority to inspect the computer by obtaining permission of the computer's owner before investigating the computer's contents. Digital records recovered in computer searches are becoming widely recognized and acceptable for use in both criminal and civil investigations. If the investigator has expert knowledge, they can attempt to recover the data themselves. If they do not, they should employ the services of a computer forensic specialist who has the expertise to recover any possible data and/or evidence.

The investigator will want to:

- Isolate the computer to ensure no one has access to it until it is examined. This includes direct and remote access.

- Identify the operating system and software utilized.

- Disable any remote access for other users.

- Either have the IT department head provide password access, reset passwords, or obtain the password from the user.

- The investigator should prepare to have the system backed up for redundancy in case files are ruined during the search.

- The investigator should be prepared to copy files and capture original screens to establish a chain of custody and document and record the retrieval of data.

- Employees or subjects of investigations should be instructed not to destroy evidence or delete files.

Methods

With the advent of advanced technology many cell phones now serve as computers. Although they may seem similar, cell phone forensics and computer forensics are very different. As a result, the laws are also different for extracting data from each type of device. Investigators should be familiar with federal and state laws governing the search of computers and cell phone devices. Cell phone protections involve additional privacy laws. Data from each can be used in criminal and civil investigations.

The investigator should be prepared to ask the client the make and model of the cell phone or computer, the identity of the registered owner, determine if the device is password protected, and if so, what the password is if known.

Preparation

Once the investigator identifies the type of device that will be searched, they can determine if the search is within their area of expertise or if they will need to identify and contract with someone with greater expertise related to the computer or device. Things for the investigator to consider are:

- Where the system is located
- Who presently has access to the computer or device

- If the device can be moved or of it must stay in the location it is presently at
- What security protections may be on the system
- If the computer or device is being searched covertly, the investigator's activities must be accomplished without others becoming aware of the search.
- The types of software that may be within the system
- Having a storage device to store copied files
- Costs associated with hiring a computer forensic specialist

Federal Criminal Statutes Related to Financial Crime

Financial crimes are set forth in federal law and qualified by federal statute. Federal prosecution of financial crimes generally falls under a higher monetary threshold than lower threshold financial crimes that may be pursued by lower courts on the state or local level. The following are federal criminal statutes that specifically prohibit financial crime:

- 18 U.S.C. 215: This defines illegal standards for officers, directors, employees, agents, or attorneys of financial institutions to solicit, demand, or accept anything of value from constituents.

- 18 U.S.C. 641: This defines illegal standards against embezzlement, stealing, purloin, or any other unauthorized use of public funds, property, or records.

- 18 U.S.C. 656: This defines illegal standards of embezzlement, theft, or misapplication by bank officers or employees.

- 18 U.S.C. 1344: This defines what constitutes financial institution frauds.

- 18 U.S.C. 1001: This prohibits knowingly making general falsified statements.

- 18 U.S.C. 1005: This provides protection against officers and employees of financial institutions making false entries, including material omissions.

- 18 U.S.C. 1014: This provides guidelines in an effort to safeguard against the creation of fraudulent loans and credit applications, renewals and discounts, and crop insurance.

- 18 U.S.C. 1341 and 1343: These prohibit fraud via mail, wire, radio, or television.

- 18 U.S.C. 2 and 371: This statute covers general offenses and fraud.

Workplace Theft and Fraud

Prevention
Workplace fraud and prevention programs cost business's millions of dollars each year. There are certain steps employers can take to reduce the risk of product shrinkage, theft of intellectual property, illegal financial transactions, and other types of workplace theft. The following are some of those safeguards:

- Employment screening: Screening the right employees with good references, a favorable credit history, and a steady employment history is the first step in safeguarding against workplace theft and fraud.

- Employment agreements: As part of the employment agreement, the employer should write in safeguards to protect the business. For example, if the employee is in a warehouse that houses small expensive bottles of perfume then the employment agreement should have as a condition of employment that the employee is subject to searches of their person and bags to prevent them from stealing perfume bottles.

- Signage: Posting signage about loss protection, posting signs stating that cameras are posted, and other security orientation will increase employee awareness to loss protection.

- Programs: Implementing best practices in loss prevention will help prevent and expose theft and fraud. Provide a confidential avenue for employees to report suspected fraud or theft.

A good security program should be implemented that is structured towards the risk associated with the business. If the employees routinely handle money, then conducting a credit history when screening candidates is a good practice. Other suggested safeguards would be camera surveillance, good written policy and procedures with checks and balances such as manager verification on random transactions, and final register reconciliations at the end of the day should all be implemented. If the information being protected is proprietary, the employer should have employees sign confidentiality agreements.

Fraudulent Behavior

According to the *Association of Certified Fraud Examiners (ACFE)*, the profile of a person who commits fraud is typically a male between the ages of 31 and 45 years of age with no prior history of fraud. In general, the higher the position of the person in the organization the higher the value the theft will be. The majority of the fraud is committed by employees in the departments of operations, sales, finance, customer service, and purchasing. Those involved in fraudulent activities can set off warning signs such as living above their means. Managers need to be trained on detection and to be on the lookout for early warning signs.

Lapping Fraud

Lapping can be described as misapplying funds from one receivable to the next. Money can be skimmed in a delay of cash application, and the employee takes some of the cash and then posts subsequent incoming cash from another account to the account they just took from. Any subsequent cash coming in goes to the following account they took from. The money is juggled, and since billing is constant, lapping is difficult to detect.

Typical Small Business Fraud

Smaller businesses generally present a greater target of opportunity because they have less standardized processes and systems due to their size, maturity, and experience. They also generally have less oversight and can deal more frequently in cash transactions than larger businesses. Some of the easiest ways for fraud to be committed is:

- Unrecorded sales: An example of an unrecorded sale would be when an exterminator who works for a business reports to an appointment and accepts cash for the job and tells the main office that the customer declined the sale. An off-hours sale can occur if the exterminator tells the customer that they can come back after hours and provide the service for a cheaper price on their own.

- False transaction: An example of a false transaction would be a grocery clerk ringing up only every third item for a friend of theirs.

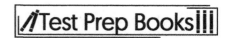

- Mail theft: Employees can intercept checks and attempt to cash them through a third party.

- Shrinkage: This happens when an employee takes products from inventory without employer's knowledge.

- Theft of service: Employees can steal time by falsifying work schedule records, submitting false receipts, etc.

Phantom Employee Fraud Investigation

Some organizations can unwittingly pay payroll costs on *ghosted* posts or posts that are supposed to be staffed but are vacant while an employee is receiving payroll for that post. This practice can go on undetected, but the investigator can begin to research this type of fraud using time sheets, work logs, surveillance cameras, staff interviews, productivity reports, and manager interviews. In cases of related theft of service fraud, employee checks can be duplicated and cashed. In other cases, employees or vendors can electronically deposit a check and then manually attempt to cash a check.

Cost/Benefit Analysis in Employee Theft

The employer should weigh the possible costs and impact of an aggressive *antifraud campaign*. Creating an atmosphere of distrust can have a negative psychological impact on employees and can be counterproductive to output. The costs of the program might also outweigh the costs of potential shrinkage and can negatively affect employee morale. Litigation is always a concern with increased exposure to violation of privacy concerns, false accusation, arrest, or negative company opinion.

Areas Most Susceptible to Employee Theft

- Expensive inventory and places where high value items are stored are desired targets for thieves.

- Garbage and garbage bags are preferred methods for theft because thieves can place the garbage outside the building and retrieve it later with the assumption no one will check the garbage.

- Secluded areas and areas that may not have camera coverage or in darker and secluded areas.

- Common areas such as lockers, bathrooms, and other common areas.

- Employee bags can be used for theft, and the employer should mandate clear plastic bags for transparency to prevent company items from being placed in employee bags.

- Bathrooms afford privacy and can be places where employees shred wrapping and conceal items because they know there are no cameras.

- Skids and pallets of product and cases of merchandise should be shrink-wrapped and sealed with security tape until needed for packing.

Employee Theft Investigation Methods

There are several ways to uncover employee theft. The most significant way is *inventory control*. A tight inventory control system will permit exposure to loss of product and will identify the type of goods missing, the area, and volume of theft. Another way to uncover employee theft is through a system of checks and balances. If security specialists check registers, products, and pallets; the search will uncover inconsistencies in product counts. Another method of detection is the spot checking of bags, persons, outgoing orders, and inventory in a random fashion to catch short orders, missing product, or employees with products on their person. Independent audits are also valuable towards identifying discrepancies.

Prevention
Some of the steps below will help prevent employee theft:

- Screening candidates for employment through background checks and credit worthiness especially for positions that will handle money and for those in positions of trust. A poor credit history may not mean a person will steal, but it will certainly provide a significant barometer for a person to steal as opposed to someone who doesn't have a bad credit history.

- Creating security awareness by having employees sign security related documents and security orientation information and attending security briefings.

- Instituting a confidential reporting system for employees to report wrongdoing without fear of being stigmatized.

- Publicizing instances of employee theft and subsequent sanctions to deter others.

- The posting of signage with security related warnings.

- Having a comprehensive surveillance system in place.

- Having comprehensive operational policies and workplace policies to avoid ambiguity in duties and responsibilities and provide clear levels of authority and permissions for employees.

Cargo Theft

Cargo Theft Investigation Techniques
Cargo is a favorable target for thieves because of the value and transiency of the product. Tight inventory control and the proper wrapping, tracking, and surveillance of the cargo will reduce the likelihood of loss. Cargo should maintain a concise inventory of not just boxes but box contents to not only track the number of boxes but also the number of products within each box. Cargo pallets should be wrapped with plastic and then sealed with a security tape which will make it obvious if it has been tampered with. Pallets of product should also be weighed to determine not only the product count but the weight which is a check and balance against someone replacing or removing a box of product from the pallet. High value products should be tracked with a GPS device.

When performing cargo theft investigations, the use of undercover investigators and/or technology to track and provide surveillance on products are techniques frequently employed by investigators. Investigators also look for those selling discounted products on the internet or other local sources which could lead back the loss of product from their client. Encouraging confidential reporting from employees can also be a good source of intelligence related to cargo theft.

Pilferage
Pilferage is the act of stealing something in small quantities or volume. Most cargo pilferage is in small volume because thieves recognize that the larger the theft the more likely it will be detected. Therefore, employees will attempt to take small, unnoticeable amounts of product generally from areas that have the least amount of surveillance and loose inventory controls. Items for shipping are generally picked

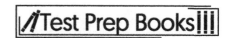

from warehouse shelves by line workers and placed in a packing room to fill an order. Once the order is filled, it is packed by packers and sent to shipping. The transport company should place the order in a secure shipping container or on a pallet with shrink wrapping and security tape.

The shipping label should identify the entire shipping contents; it should identify who picked the order, who packed the order, and the two persons who independently verified the order. The bill of lading or shipping order should contain the seal number to make sure it wasn't switched along with a detailed list of the inventory and should contain signatures to verify the information on the product type and volume.

Cargo Theft Report

If there is a product loss from the cargo, the investigator should try to obtain as much information as possible surrounding the loss. Below is some of the specific cargo related information that the investigator should seek:

- The identification of the pickers, packers, and shippers at the location of origin.

- The types and identification numbers of transport vehicles or vessels used in transport and the names of all those on the vehicles or vessels that had access.

- The destination of the product and all way points the product traveled through to reach its destination.

- The bill of lading or shipping invoice.

- The dates and times of product transfer and identification of which location or locations are under camera surveillance.

- Information on the loss discovery such as who reported it, when it was reported, how it was reported, what loss was reported, and why the product may have been a target.

- Cargo theft can involve employees so a comprehensive list of all employees and vendors who may have been exposed to the product just prior to its loss should be compiled.

- A review of any technology employed in the tracking of the product just prior to loss such as GPS tracking, camera surveillance, weigh station reports, etc.

Marine Cargo Movement Procedures

When cargo is transported by a water vessel the following procedures usually accompany the shipment:

- The carrier, tender, or transporter receives a list of the ship's expected cargo. The buyer or receiver of the cargo is then notified by the carrier on when to expect the shipment.

- The buyer or broker between the two parties clears the shipment through the United States Department of Agriculture if coming from a foreign shore, and when approval is received, they confirm the trucking or rail transport company assigned to transport the product to its final destination.

- Upon transport approval, the land-based transport company coordinates with the water-based shipping company on cargo pickup times and location.

- When the land-based transport company retrieves the goods for transport, they may be required to have a customs identification card issued by the United States Customs and Border Patrol.

- The driver presents their credentials to the terminal security and if approved is directed to United States Customs.

- United States Customs verifies the pickup and credentials and upon approval authorizes the driver to proceed to the pickup.

- The terminal operator directs the driver to the product shipment where it is loaded after verification against the shipping order or bill of lading with verification by the terminal operator and the land-based carrier. A copy is given to United States Customs.

- The land-based carrier is then free to transport the shipment.

Air Cargo Movement Procedures

Air cargo is generally received at international airports that can support air cargo transport operations. All foreign products must be cleared by several government agencies to protect their respective interests. These could include the U.S. Department of Agriculture, U.S. Customs, the U.S. Department of Health, or the FBI among others. Air cargo transport procedures require similar U.S. Customs transport procedures as defined for water-based transports. Prior to arrival of the product, it must have been cleared by U.S. Customs at the point of entry and any other governing authority at the point of departure.

Property Pass

Employees, vendors, and purchasers may be issued a property pass which is a written authorization to remove an item from a secure location. The intent of the property pass is to provide authorization for the removal of an item and to provide a record of the item or items removed. This will prevent unauthorized items from leaving the premises and keep track of permitted items to leave. The property pass should list:

- The items being removed
- The person who authorized the items to be removed with the date of approval
- The date and time of removal
- The identification of the person taking the items along with any related vehicle information

The pass should be in written or electronic form, on a standardized and recognized pass document, and should require signatures for verification of items received. There should be a filing system of the documents for review and record keeping.

Undercover Workplace Investigations

Undercover Employee Theft Investigations

Common tactics of undercover operatives in the workplace are:

- Embedding an operative that can blend in well with the employees. For example, if theft is suspected from a factory that has a predominant Hispanic employee population that packs and

ships small perfume bottles, the undercover should be a Spanish speaking operative in the same age group as the majority of the other employees in order to blend in.

- The operative must go deep undercover and act just like the other employees. In order to minimize exposure, the investigator should not report on activities while working in the undercover role. Furthermore, the undercover investigator/operative should have a system set up to covertly report to the investigation supervisor and guarantee that investigator meeting locations are far away from the workplace.

- The true identity of the investigator and the covert investigation must not be exposed. The investigator must work out a system with management beforehand where the investigator can alert management to intercept an offending person without making it look like there is a "rat" in the employee's midst.

- An undercover can also pose as a buyer of goods and can try to attract those engaged in illegal activity.

- The undercover should try to build up a rapport with employees to make them feel comfortable enough to speak about related activity.

- The undercover should be given a position that permits maximum observation within the organization.

- The undercover officer should have experience, a good cover story or credentials, and research the environment they are entering beforehand.

Preparation
In order to execute a favorable undercover operation, the following preparatory steps should be taken:

- The client must provide a concise briefing on the length and objective of the operation. This briefing must pay particular attention to who in the organization will know about the operation and how the undercover operative will be processed for hiring and payroll to look like a current employee. It should also be known prior to the assignment what job the undercover will be assigned to.

- There should be an assigned client contact, someone from within the organization that communicates with the undercover officer. The method and frequency of communication must be established beforehand. It can be a phone check in, text exchange, meeting at previously established intervals, or whatever works best for the information flow.

- There should be prior discussion on what types of actions if any will force the undercover to blow their cover and take immediate action. In most cases the undercover officer should have a way to report out illegal activity as it occurs to other company management employees who can intercept the illegal activity themselves; this independent company action will maintain the undercover officer's covert role.

- Business operations should remain as usual when integrating the undercover officer. If actions or procedures are implemented to prepare for the undercover officer, it may appear suspicious to company employees.

Involvement of Law Enforcement Agents

Criminal investigations involving the use of undercover officers will not generally involve private security officers. The law enforcement agency will keep the identity of undercover officers confidential except in cases where company management must assist by providing credentials or access to aid an undercover police operation.

In non-criminal undercover operations, covert surveillance is generally geared towards loss prevention activities and may involve criminal prosecution after the undercover operation exposes criminal activity that is presented to law enforcement.

Legal Oversight

Since undercover operations involve privacy issues related to observation and search, it is a good practice to involve the firm's general counsel or outside legal counsel for consultation. Lawyers will be knowledgeable regarding federal, state, and local laws as it relates to undercover operations. Legal counsel can also provide guidance to the investigator if the case involves a litigation response related to the undercover operation.

Substance Abuse Investigations

Many employers have a substance abuse policy as a condition of employment or as part of the employment agreement. If an investigator is called in for a workplace substance abuse investigation, they should become familiar with the organization's substance abuse policy. The following should be considered in substance abuse investigations.

- If the employee consented to the substance policy as a condition of employment in their employment agreement, then the investigator can follow the provisions of that policy.

- In many cases a simple hunch that someone is under the influence is not enough to order a substance screening or take disciplinary action. The action or behavior must be observed and then supported by an independent observation or review.

- In many organizations the ordered substance testing must be approved by the general counsel.

- If the organization has a random substance screening policy, then the employee must cooperate and yield a bodily fluid sample as stipulated by the organization's substance testing policy.

- The organization might have a zero-tolerance policy or a redemptive policy of treatment for first offenders.

The private investigation agency must ensure the organization's substance abuse policy is followed, and the policy must provide the due process to the employee under suspicion.

Shoplifting

Shoplifting causes retailers millions of dollars in losses each year. There are many reasons why people shoplift: personal need, to support a dependency on drugs, to satisfy psychological problems, black market sales, or as a rite of passage for juveniles. Items that are shoplifted can range from meats in a grocery store to personal hygiene products. Shoplifting can be countered by deterrence through signage, overt surveillance cameras, uniformed guards, and safeguarding small expense items in

controlled secure boxes or placed behind the register. Covert methods include the use of undercover operatives, covert surveillance cameras, and tracking devices placed on expensive merchandise.

Shoplifter Profiles

Shoplifters come in all ages, genders, races, and social classes. There is no hard and fast profile of a shoplifter, but the following are some signs that may raise red flags and support further investigation:

- Individuals carrying bags
- Individuals that look suspicious or that are looking around to see if they are being watched
- Individuals that are involved in creating a distraction and may be working in conjunction with another shoplifter
- Individuals who take a lot of clothes into a dressing room and don't come out with them
- Individuals in groups who don't appear to be seriously shopping
- Individuals who appear disinterested in the items they are looking at

Loss Prevention

Detecting shoplifting is difficult and requires a comprehensive plan to deter shoplifting. The following suggestions could reduce shoplifting:

- Post signage warning potential shoplifters that the store is monitored.

- If the security budget permits, hire uniformed and undercover security officers.

- Post overt cameras and covert camera surveillance for deterrence and detection.

- Place expensive items close to employee supervision or in areas of high visibility for natural surveillance.

- Employ the use of tracking devices on expensive items.

- Prohibit outside packages from coming into the store.

- Have employees use clear plastic bags for their personal belongings to prevent them from putting store products in their bags.

- Place mirrors around the store to increase visibility.

- Maintain tight control on garments being brought into fitting rooms.

- Require employees to greet each person walking into the store for observation.

- Require cashiers to check every item sold that might hide stolen items within it.

Auto Theft Claim Assessment

Auto theft is a criminal charge, and the private investigator may be involved in the investigation along with the police. When conducting auto theft investigations, some things for an investigator to consider are:

- The last know location of the vehicle
- The registered owner

- The persons who had access to the vehicle
- The tag number, registration number, vehicle make and model, and color of the vehicle
- Any surveillance footage from the adjacent areas of loss
- If any tracking devices are on the vehicle
- The lien holder if any
- The approximate value of the vehicle
- Check local listings for the sale of possible stolen parts that correlate to the vehicle theft
- The insurance company involved
- The owner's history of loss claims
- Any possible financial motive

Fuel Theft Investigation

In order to determine appropriate fuel use among company vehicles, many organizations utilize a fleet vendor or software program that tracks fuel use. The system provides each authorized operator with a fuel card that correlates to a vehicle and assigns a pin number for each registered driver. This system can track the fuel use by driver or by car and provides specific reports on usage. The usage report can provide the average miles per gallon per vehicle, can provide exceptions to predetermined thresholds for use, and can easily detect fuel theft.

Employers can set estimate ranges on how much fuel a vehicle in the fleet should use weekly and how much a driver should use. If thresholds are breached, then a notification will be sent to management for review. Some vehicles can also be outfitted with GPS monitoring which can identify idle time, location, movement, and establish a geo fence with alerts if a driver goes outside of a predetermined geographical footprint.

Workplace Violence

Workplace violence is unfortunately becoming more common and has recently manifested itself into national headlines. All threats of workplace violence whether direct, implied, or third party must be taken seriously and investigated thoroughly. Upon learning of a threat of workplace violence local police should be notified even if an investigator is already involved. The following actions should also be considered:

- An immediate investigation should be commenced.

- If a direct threat or implied threat was communicated by the employee or any other condition exists which suggests that violence in the workplace has occurred or is imminent then the police should be immediately notified.

- Consider if the employee violated a workplace policy or condition of employment and consider placing the employee on leave or reassigning to a different area while the investigation is ongoing.

- Consider enhanced security staffing and restricting workplace access until the outcome of the investigation.

- Check surveillance cameras, interview witnesses, and review reports to determine any additional information that might aid the investigation.

- All information should be documented to support the investigative findings and to defend against any subsequent litigation.

- All employees involved should receive in-service workplace violence training and policy guidelines to reinforce the organizations policy against workplace violence.

Sexual Discrimination and Harassment Investigations

Sexual discrimination and harassment are prohibited in the workplace by both federal and state regulations. Investigators are often called upon to investigate claims of sexual harassment or discrimination. While doing so, the investigator should be aware that retaliation against any complainant of sexual discrimination or harassment can be viewed worse than the original harassment offense.

The investigator should start the investigation with a review of the background or history of the subject of the complaint, and then conduct an interview to determine all the facts and circumstances of the complaint. The investigator should then interview all known and potential witnesses and review all evidence such as texts, emails, phone recordings, and any other hard evidence to support or refute the claim. After completing the investigation, the investigator should determine if the allegation is confirmed, unfounded, or inconclusive.

Due Diligence Investigations

Due diligence is a term often used by businesses or attorneys to indicate a comprehensive search and review to determine the integrity, history, worthiness, and past performance of a person or business they are scheduled to transact with. The objective is to determine if the person or business is in good stead and has the financial means to act reliably in a business transaction. The main focus is to determine the financial integrity, but a due diligence search usually extends to the person or business's performance history as well.

It can incorporate a wide range of search material to include internet searches, credit history searches, Dun and Bradstreet reviews, licensing complaints, BBB complaints, audits of profit and loss statements and bank records, request for third party lending information, a review of liens and actions against the company or person, and any other review which will provide the investigator with a comprehensive summary of the financial integrity of the person or business they are set to engage with.

Arson

Arson is a crime involving a fire that is intentionally set. There are many motives for setting a fire:

- To eliminate the evidence of a crime
- To intentionally kill or injure others
- Insurance gain if the property has more value in insurance that it would in an actual sale
- To satisfy the ego of a pyromaniac
- To satisfy the heroic need of a rescue worker who might set the fire to later be viewed as a hero involved in the rescue
- Revenge, extortion, or marital disputes

Arson should be suspected in cases where:

- An accelerant is found at the scene of the fire.

- Items of value appear staged at the scene to increase the value of the loss.

- A possible motive for a crime is present or actual evidence of a crime is discovered.

- The fire damage appears to have originated in an unlikely place and spread more quickly than anticipated.

- The property is the subject of dispute, sale, or other legal action.

- There is evidence of exclusive access.

- A hunch by the investigator that something may seem unusual or suspicious about the circumstances or behavior of those involved in the fire is present.

Arson investigators are trained experts often called in by fire personnel after concluding suspicious circumstances exist surrounding the fire. Their training permits them to collect evidence and evaluate circumstances to determine if a crime was committed at the scene of a fire. If the fire is determined to be suspicious, it should immediately be made a crime scene to preserve evidence until the arson investigators complete their work.

If a private investigator is involved in a fire investigation, then certain actions should be implemented:

- Set up or maintain a crime scene until it has been cleared by police or arson investigators in an effort to preserve evidence.

- Record the crowd, if possible, outside a fire scene as many arsonists or those criminally involved in the fire may return to the scene to observe the aftermath.

- Record the names, badge numbers, and agencies of all responding emergency personnel, especially those of supervisors.

- Record the names and contact information of all witnesses and potential witnesses at the scene.

- Identify the time of the fire response call, determine who made the call, and record the time the first responders came on the scene to help establish a time line.

- Determine if any internal or external surveillance cameras in the area permit an internal and external view of the building or surrounding blocks just prior to the fire.

- Compile a list of all persons who may have had access to the site.

- Take photos or identify which responding agency took photos which can later be used for investigative purposes.

- Conduct initial interviews to determine the facts related to the fire investigation.

- Review histories of those closest to the circumstances of the arson to determine patterns of behavior or motive that may be consistent with the motive for arson.

Burglary

Many people confuse burglary and robbery. The easiest way to remember the difference is that a robbery involves theft to a person while burglary involves breaking into a private residence or business. Burglary can be classified into several different categories based upon the jurisdiction it occurs in. Burglaries can be classified with or without weapons. Burglaries can also be classified as occupied or unoccupied burglaries depending whether there are persons in the premises when it is burglarized. Burglary motivated by the need to accomplish another crime can be classified along with the intended crime. The mere possession of recognized burglary tools can also trigger an arrest for possession of burglary related materials. It should be noted most criminals have a "M.O." or Modus Operandi or method of operation, and burglars are no different.

When investigating burglaries some of the most important things to consider are:

- The investigator should ensure the preservation of any evidence at the crime scene.

- The investigators should determine if there are any surveillance cameras in the location or the surrounding blocks or area.

- If the burglary occurred at a place that has some form of access control, then the access control records and surveillance should be reviewed.

- The investigator should determine the approximate day and time of the loss.

- The investigator should take photos and take inventory of the items of loss that the victim or victims can recall. If possible, they should obtain serial numbers and identification marks that may help locate the stolen items at a later date.

- The investigator should determine if any security protocols were bypassed.

- The investigator should investigate persons who may have recently had access to the property such as those hired for services who may have knowledge of the layout and contents.

- The investigator should determine if the burglary looked like a random crime of opportunity of if the burglary was planned and staged.

- The investigator should make a comprehensive list of all of those who may have information on the burglary and who may be potential witnesses. Also, the investigator should interview anyone with access to the premises for whatever information they may be able to provide.

Robbery

Robbery is the forcible taking of money or property from another individual by force or intimidation with the clear intent to deprive them of that money or property. Robbery can differ by location and can differ by accompanying circumstances that are generally classified into *degrees*. First degree robbery for example is the most serious and may involve high value items or violence. Third degree robbery would be a lesser crime with less value given to the stolen property. A lesser degree of robbery might also be classified downward to larceny which is considered a less serious offense.

Besides being classified into varying degrees, robberies can also be classified based upon the mitigating circumstances of the robbery or intent. The classifications could vary by jurisdiction, but common examples of those classifications are armed robbery, unarmed robbery, robbery with intent to commit another crime, and larceny.

If investigating a robbery or larceny, the following are steps an investigator should consider:

- The location, date, and time of the robbery

- A review of surveillance cameras both in and around the location of the crime

- A review of access control areas to the location of the crime

- A canvas and interview of potential witnesses

- An interview with the subject of the theft

- Any description or identifying features of the robbers should be identified and broadcast to the police as soon as possible

- Collection of any evidence that is available

- The determination of the item or items taken and the determination of a possible motive

- To determine if this was a crime of opportunity or if the victim was targeted

- If a vehicle was involved, then vehicle descriptions and tag numbers should be identified if possible.

Sex Related Crime Investigations

Sex related crime investigations are generally handled by police when it is identified that a sex crime has been committed. Because of the sensitivity of victims of sex crimes, many police agencies have a special victims unit that is trained to deal with the confidentiality and sensitivity associated with sex crime investigations. Investigators can investigate suspected sex related offenses, but when evidence of a sex related crime is uncovered, they should make a notification to law enforcement.

With the advent of the internet, computers can prove both as a catalyst for sex related offenses and as a useful tool for catching sex offenders. In the course of suspected sex related offenses, the following are some things the investigator may consider in addition to the routine investigative procedures previously outlined:

- Research of local laws related to sexual offenses and privacy
- Identify the ages of potential victims
- Consider if parental consent is needed for the interview of minors
- Search local sex offender registries
- Consider the preservation of evidence especially DNA and computer related files and photographs of injuries
- Consider referrals for medical services
- Maintain strict confidentiality and sensitivity
- Consider gender specific interviewing
- Consider notification to police if warranted

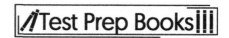

Hate Crime

Many police jurisdictions now classify crimes targeted against specific groups as hate crimes. Penalties associated with hate crimes can be generally more severe in order to offer a greater deterrence against hate crimes to prevent crimes against protected classes. To be classified as a hate crime there must be evidence that the victim was targeted because of bias against their gender, race, religion, sexual orientation, nationality, or any other recognized bias.

Evidence could be as simple as a perpetrator using a racial epithet during an assault or spraying anti-Semitic graffiti on a wall. Motivation for committing hate crimes is wide ranging but fortunately the advent of stricter laws and stiffer penalties act as a strong deterrent against hate crimes. If the investigator is pursuing a possible hate crime investigation, they should review all evidence that may support a bias related connection in conjunction with similar patterns of related crime or suspected crime in the same geographical area. Any evidence that supports a hate crime should be reported to the local police with supporting evidence presented by the investigator who collected it.

Gray and Counterfeit Goods Investigations

"Gray goods" is a term that refers to products that an organization sells to a distributor or other party at a deep discount for sale in a country or place that would command a lower price for the product and that product makes its way back into United States shelves at a price lower than retail. Depending upon the circumstances, prosecution against the sale of gray goods may be upheld or denied depending on the circumstances, contract provisions between parties, and protections offered under the related provisions of the US Code.

Counterfeit products are illegal versions of copyrighted retail products than in most cases are copycatted overseas and sold for a fraction of the price in the United States. Counterfeiting most commonly involves products such as handbags, watches, expensive clothing, shoes, and first run movies. Corporations work vigorously to thwart counterfeit operations and may enlist the assistance of a private investigator for surveillance, decoy, and case preparation. Some counterfeit operations can be prosecuted federally, and the investigator should consult with police agencies regarding the vicinity of where the investigations are taking place.

Constructive and Reconstructive Investigations

Constructive investigations are proactive in that they involve the pursuit of evidence collection, surveillance, and interviews to determine if and when a crime will occur with the intent to either prevent it or run parallel to catch it when it occurs.

A *reconstructive investigation* by contrast is reactionary and occurs in response to a criminal act. The goal of the reconstructive investigation is to determine what factually transpired by essentially working backwards from the results of the crime to the circumstances that led up to the crime.

Practice Questions

1. Which of the following circumstances would be a major ethical violation for an attorney?
   a. Maintaining strict confidentiality of information received from their client even if asked by a judge.
   b. Not reporting a conflict of interest that in the attorney's opinion won't affect the outcome of the case.
   c. Not attempting to unduly influence judges or court personnel to try to win the case.
   d. Protecting client's funds safely from others.

2. When a private investigator conducting a workplace related investigation comes across a complaint of discrimination the most appropriate course of action for them would be to:
   a. Notify the police.
   b. If the complaint does not relate to the investigation then the investigator should ignore it.
   c. Notify management of the organization involved and/or their client.
   d. Instruct the employee to file a complaint with state of federal EEO board.

3. Which of the following best describes the Alternative Dispute Resolution process or "ADR"?
   a. It is part of the US Code and must be followed in all federal cases.
   b. It is the legislation that formed the Federal Mediation and Conciliation Service.
   c. It is a mechanism employed by arbitrators to try to settle disputes by any means outside of the courtroom.
   d. All of the above are true

4. Which of the following is <u>NOT</u> true in reference to appointing an arbitrator to a labor dispute consistent with the Administrative Dispute Resolution Act of 1996?
   a. The appointed arbitrator must be a person that is agreeable to both parties.
   b. The arbitrator must not have a conflict of interest in the case they are hearing. If they do, they must state it to both parties who must agree to proceed despite the conflict of interest.
   c. The arbitrator cannot be replaced by either side once the Administrative Dispute Resolution process begins.
   d. The arbitrator should have conflict resolution experience and come from a specialized agency that deals in negotiations.

5. In reference to franchise disputes, which of the following statements is true?
   a. The court can order mediation for parties involved in franchise disputes under the Federal Rules of Civil Procedure Law.
   b. The court does not have the right to order mediation for parties involved in franchise disputes.
   c. Federal Rules of Civil Procedure Law do not apply to franchise disputes.
   d. None of the above statements are true

6. Which of the following statements is most accurate about the notes of a private investigator?
   a. They are not admissible in court.
   b. They are admissible in court.
   c. In order to be admissible in court they must be signed by the witness.
   d. In order to be used in court they need to be signed by the investigator.

7. Which of the following statements is true in relation to pre-employment investigations?
   a. The investigator must have the prospective employee's consent.
   b. The investigator does not need the prospective employee's consent.
   c. If the prospective employee is applying for the job, the signed application itself gives permission for a background investigation.
   d. The employer can order a pre-employment investigation if the employer determines a concern exists with the candidate's application.

8. Which of the following provides the best definition of "Pilferage"?
   a. Burglary
   b. Robbery
   c. Petty theft
   d. Counterfeiting products

9. Which of the following is NOT an effective workplace fraud prevention program?
   a. Employment screening
   b. Signage warning of consequences for stealing company merchandise.
   c. Posting signs indicating an area is under surveillance.
   d. Notifying employees of which shifts a security guard will be undercover on.

10. Duplicating a driver's license on a computer is an example of which type of computer crime?
    a. Computer forgery
    b. Computer fraud manipulation
    c. Computer unauthorized access
    d. None of the above

11. Which of the following is true about the rules of privileged communication?
    a. If it is told to a third party, then the confidentiality is breached, and it is no longer privileged communication.
    b. It cannot be waived even if both parties agree.
    c. It does not apply to a husband and wife.
    d. If it takes place in a public setting with no reasonable expectation of privacy it still can remain privileged.

12. According to the Association of Certified Fraud Examiners (ACFE) the profile of a person who commits fraud is typically?
    a. A juvenile 16-18 years of age.
    b. A female 18-24 years of age.
    c. A male adult 31-45 years of age.
    d. There is no profile of a person who commits fraud.

13. Which of the following is LEAST LIKELY to aid an investigator who is investigating a cargo related theft?

a. The identification of the pickers, packers, and shippers at the location of origin.

b. The types and identification numbers of transport vehicles or vessels used in transport and the names of all those on the vehicles or vessels that had access.

c. The destination of the product and all way points the product traveled through to reach its destination.

d. Interviews with the intended recipients of the product or merchandise who had not yet received the merchandise.

14. Which of the following is the best practice or practices to help prevent employee theft?

a. Screening employment candidates.

b. Providing a security orientation to new employees.

c. Having a system of checks and balances and frequent audits and reviews based around comprehensive policies and procedures for employees to follow.

d. All of the above are best practices which if implemented will prevent employee theft.

15. Which of the following is the best description of a robbery?

a. Breaking into someone's apartment

b. Breaking into someone's apartment and taking money

c. Asking someone for their wallet while holding a weapon

d. Taking someone's car while they are not in it

Answer Explanations

1. B: An attorney must report any conflict of interest even if they don't think it will affect the outcome of the case because others could argue differently, and it could void the case. Choice *A* is incorrect because the attorney must maintain confidentiality according to attorney–client privilege, and the privilege protection applies to the judge as well. Choice *C* is incorrect because the attorney is not permitted to unduly influence judges or court personnel. Choice *D* is incorrect because an attorney has a fiduciary responsibility to keep client funds safe if entrusted to them.

2. C: The investigator has an obligation to report wrongdoing. Choice *A* is incorrect because discrimination is not a crime so the police are not required to be notified. Choice *B* is incorrect because an investigator is not obligated to report all wrong doing or allegations of wrong doing to their client. Choice *D* is incorrect because it is the complainant's responsibility to make an EEO notification outside the organization if they choose to do so.

3. C: Choice *A* is incorrect because the ADR is not part of the U.S. Code. Choice *B* is incorrect because the ADR is a process not legislation. Choice *D* is incorrect because if *A* and *B*. are incorrect then Choice *D* must also be incorrect.

4. C: Choice *C* is correct because, according to the rules of the ADR process, either side can have an arbitrator replaced at any time upon request. Choice *A* is incorrect because both parties must agree upon the arbitrator. Choice *B* is incorrect because the arbitrator must not have any conflict of interest which may influence them to one side over the other. Choice *D* is incorrect because according to the Administrative Dispute Resolution Act of 1996 the arbitrator should have conflict resolution experience and come from a specialized agency that deals in negotiations.

5. A: Choice *A* is correct because the court has decided that because there is such a high volume of franchise disputes, the court can order mediation for parties involved in a franchise dispute under the Federal Rules of Civil Procedure law. Choices *B* and *C* are incorrect because if Choice *A* is correct then it automatically invalidates Choices *B* and *C* which are the opposite of Choice *A*. Choice *D* is also invalid because *A* is the correct answer which rules out "None of the above are true" as a valid answer.

6: B: Choice *B* is correct as courts can subpoena the notes of investigators as evidence, and investigators can submit them as part of discovery in a case. If Choice *B* is correct, then it automatically invalidates Choice *A*. Choice *C* is incorrect because a witness is not required to validate the investigator's notes. Choice *D* is incorrect because the investigator need not sign the notes because if they are introduced in court the investigator can identify the notes and establish their authenticity.

7. A: Choice *A* is correct because in order to perform a pre-employment investigation the investigator must have the prospective employee's consent, otherwise they may be violating privacy laws. Choice *B* is incorrect by virtue of Choice *A* being correct. Choice *C* is incorrect because a signed application does not give consent for a pre-employment investigation unless it specifically states that. Choice *D* is incorrect because the candidate's permission is required.

8. C: Choice *C* is correct because petty theft is the taking of small items. Choice *A* is incorrect because it involves taking an item of value from a residence which is burglary. Choice *B* is incorrect because it involves taking something from a person which is robbery. Choice *D* is incorrect because counterfeiting products while illegal has nothing to do with petty theft.

9. D: Choice *D* is the best choice, because if you tell employees when you will have a security guard undercover, they will then know when someone *will not* be undercover. A better approach would be to inform them that on some shifts there will be a security guard undercover so that they are never sure whether it will be on their shift. Choices *A*, *B*, and C are all good methods for fraud prevention. Good employment screening will keep potential thieves out of the workplace (Choice *A*), and signage will deter overall theft (Choice *B*). Choice *C* will have the same effect as Choice *B*.

10. A: Choice A is correct because based upon their excellent copying ability, computers are used for the illicit purpose to make fake government documents such as licenses, visas, checks, counterfeit money, and other false documents. Choice *B* is incorrect because computer fraud manipulation involves using the computer to change a document or create an action for gain and not to duplicate an exact document. Choice *C* is incorrect because unauthorized access doesn't mean the user will use the illicit computer entry to duplicate a document. Choice *D* is incorrect by virtue of Choice *A* being the correct answer.

11. A: Choice *A* is correct because once one of the parties of the privileged communication tells a third party then the privilege is broken. Choice *B* is incorrect because if both parties agree to release the information then it can be lawfully revealed. Choice *C* is incorrect because privilege does in fact apply to a husband and wife. Choice *D* is incorrect because if the persons covered by the privilege speak in a public place and are overheard then the court has determined they are not entitled to confidentiality because there was no reasonable expectation of privacy.

12. C: Choice *C* is correct based upon research provided by the Association of Certified Fraud Examiners (ACFE). If Choice *C* is correct then it invalidates Choices *A*, *B*, and *D*.

13. D: Choice *D* is correct because conducting interviews with the intended recipients of the products would not provide any direct information to assist the investigation because the recipients never received the cargo. Choices *A*, *B*, and *C* are more likely to aid an investigator; therefore, they are incorrect.

14. D: Choice *D* is correct because Choices *A*, *B*, and *C* are all good practices to prevent employee theft.

15. C: Choice *C* is correct because robbery is the forcible taking of money or property from another individual by force or intimidation with the clear intent to deprive them of that money or property. Choices *A* and *B* are examples of burglary which is a crime against a premise, and Choice *C* provides an example of vehicle theft not robbery.

Conducting Interviews & Research

Conducting Interviews

Interviews

One of the most important ways for an investigator to determine facts and circumstances surrounding an investigation that they are conducting is through interviews. Interviews can be described as a conversation in which the interviewer asks a series of questions to determine what may have happened at the scene of an investigation. The interview should not be confrontational, and investigators should treat the person being interviewed with respect and not be accusatory or threaten the subject. The primary goal of the interview is to make the subject feel comfortable with the line of questioning so that they are as cooperative and as informative as possible. Before the interview, the investigator should try to determine some of the facts of the event to question the subject about. This will allow the investigator to compare the subject's answers against what is known to be factual, in order to determine how accurate the subject's recollection of the events is.

Stages of the Interview
The stages of an interview can be categorized as follows:

- *Preparation*: The interviewer should prepare for the interview by determining beforehand the information they are trying to obtain, and then either mentally preparing or writing down notes on questions to ask, to make sure they cover all the questions they intend to. If possible, the interviewer should gain some knowledge on the subject beforehand.

- *Introduction*: The interviewer should greet the subject and introduce themselves first. The interviewer should explain that the goal of the interview is to get the subject's version of events and try to make them feel as comfortable as possible.

- *Initial rapport building*: Before going directly into a line of questioning, the interviewer should build a rapport with the subject by discussing something unrelated. The interviewer should not appear eager to be interested in specific details of the investigation only, and not the person being interviewed. The more comfortable the subject feels, the more information they may reveal.

- *Interview commencement*: The interviewer should start the interview by asking the subject to state in their own words what they saw or experienced. This is not the time to stop them or contradict anything that may be different than what another witness has said. The interviewer should not ask any leading questions that might shape the subject's answers. The interviewer should take notes if possible, and let the subject speak freely.

- *Direct line of questioning*: Once the subject has provided some initial information, the interviewer should proceed with direct questions to help clarify inconsistencies from other witnesses, which may lead the investigator to understand things that were still unclear.

- *Closing*: The interviewer should leave the lines of communication open. When ending an interview, it is a good idea to ask the subject if it is acceptable to call or contact them again if there are any follow-up questions. The subject should be given information on how to reach the

investigator in the event they remember anything that may be pertinent or if they obtain any new information. The interviewer should summarize the subject's statements. This illustrates the interviewer's understanding of the information the subject has provided. Finally, the interviewer should thank the subject for their time. The investigator should let the subject know that the information they were able to provide is appreciated and will be kept extremely confidential.

Types

Interviews generally fit into the following categories:

- *Witness interview*: This type of interview is the questioning of persons who may have seen, heard, or witnessed something that may be related to the investigation. The sooner a witness is interviewed, the better they may be able to recollect what they have witnessed.

- *Suspect interview*: This is the questioning of someone who could be the target of the investigation. It may be best to interview them last—after information has been gathered from witnesses—so that the investigator can confront the subject with some facts. The investigator is not required to read a suspect the Miranda Warning; only a sworn law enforcement officer acting in the official capacity of their duties is obligated to do so.

- *Victim interview*: In this case, there usually is a victim being investigated. That victim could suffer from a physical injury, financial loss, or other traumatic experiences. Because of that victimization, the interviewer should be sensitive to those concerns and exercise extreme patience, empathy, and compassion for the victim.

- *Informant interview*: There are a number of reasons informants provide information to an investigation. The interviewer should rate the information received based upon the reliability of the informant in the past. In all cases, the investigator must keep the confidentiality of the informant secure.

- *Ordinary citizen interview*: This pertains to the questioning of individuals not directly related to the event under investigation but who may have indirect information that might lead to other avenues of investigation.

Interview Code of Ethics

The principles of the Interview Code of Ethics are as follows. The investigator should:

- Present themselves honestly and professionally to the subject being interviewed.

- Maintain an impartial opinion, to avoid being drawn to preconceived notions.

- Honor the need by certain subjects for confidentiality, to maintain their safety.

- Treat all interview subjects with respect.

- Avoid employing intimidation, coercion, or threats of force.

- Follow federal, state, and local guidelines as they may pertain to interview techniques and the recording or videotaping of interviews.

- Be cognizant and respectful of religious beliefs, gender, sexual orientation, handicaps, economic status, and any type of minority group.

- Never accept money or other compensation that could be challenged as having prejudiced the investigation.

- Never defend both opposing parties in an investigation.

- Avoid using foul language or disparaging other persons interviewed, law enforcement, oversight agencies, or any other person or group.

Successful Interviews

Successful interviews should be conducted based on the following guidelines. The interviewer should:

- Treat the subject with respect and dignity, first and foremost.

- Understand that just as all people are not the same, interview techniques should vary based upon what strategy might elicit the best response from the subject.

- Consider the convenience of the subject, such as the best time for them to accommodate the interview, the most convenient location, if possible, and any other reasonable accommodation that might help the subject open up.

- Refrain from critiquing subjects and others in the investigation; this might cause the person being interviewed to withhold information for fear of judgment.

- Make the interview process positive by exuding a confidence and comfort level that will set the subject at ease.

- Hide emotions, to not influence the information being provided by the subject.

- Observe body language, restlessness, and other signs that the subject may be withholding information.

- Consider using long pauses as a means of compelling the subject to fill in the void with statements and be cognizant that changing the pace of the interview may be beneficial to producing the best results.

- Ask questions different ways to determine if the subject answers consistently.

- Put out unconfirmed information to gauge the subject's response; this is a useful and lawful technique.

- Be up-to-date on technology as it relates to the current investigation. If not current, the interviewer should seek further resources or training to enhance their skills or ask the advice of an expert in that technology.

- Be knowledgeable on local laws and guidelines in the jurisdiction in which they are operating, as investigations can involve legal issues, and on occasion, cross over into criminal investigation.

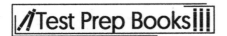

Interview Location and Comfort

Many people, even if they are not the target of an investigation, feel nervous about speaking to an investigator. It is important to set the subject at ease, and to permit them to speak freely and comfortably. The investigator should keep this in mind when coordinating the time and location of the interview. The investigator should also address concerns for confidentiality and try various techniques to alleviate any hesitation the subject may have about speaking to them. The following are some of the prerequisites for a successful interview:

- The subject should be interviewed by only one investigator, so as not to make them feel intimidated.

- If the subject is a female, then a female observer should be in the room to avoid any allegations of misconduct.

- The door to the room where the interview is being conducted should not be locked; doing so might make the subject feel as if they are under arrest.

- The exit should be clear, and the subject should feel they are free to leave at any time.

- The distance between investigator and subject should be close enough to easily communicate and observe body language, but it should not be invasive.

Interview Questions

Questions to Elicit Information
The following types of questions are recommended during an interview:

- *Pointed question*: A pointed question is very direct. Instead of asking a subject, "Have you ever used drugs?" the investigator might jump to the assumption that the subject uses drugs and ask the pointed question, "How often do you use drugs?"

- *Speculative question*: A speculative question is asking a subject to give their opinion on something hypothetical that would provide the investigator some insight into the subject's beliefs and values.

- *Placating questions*: Placating questions downplay the seriousness of an event in order to elicit information from the subject. For instance, an interviewer might say, "We have all stolen something at one time or another" to get the subject to think that they will be understood if they admit to stealing or witnessing others steal.

Direct Questioning
Direct questioning techniques are as follows. The interviewer should:

- Speak slowly, clearly, and make sure the subject comprehends what is being asked by clarifying any ambiguity.

- Resist asking multiple questions in the same statement. The interviewer should ask one direct question, let the subject respond, and then ask the next question.

- Avoid leading questions. Avoid questions that would alter the subject's account of an event or be suggestive, such as, "How fast was the truck going when it hit the SUV?" This is a leading question because it assumes that the accident was the fault of the truck driver. A better example would be, "How fast do you think the truck and SUV were going when they approached each other?" Leading questions are undesirable because they can cause the subject to provide false or slanted information.

- Ask questions that may have multiple answers and permit the subject to expound. An example is asking, "Who do you think might have a motive to commit this offense?" and letting the subject walk through the possibilities based upon their knowledge and observations.

- Display a strong interest in the responses of the subject even if they are not what the investigator wants to hear. This interest on the part of the investigator might encourage the subject to loosen up and possibly elaborate, which may permit the investigator to get the information they desire.

- Avoid using police terms, acronyms, or investigative jargon. An interviewer should always try to speak on the level of the person being interviewed.

Questions to Encourage Cooperation

The line of questioning below is best suited to gain cooperation during an interview. The interviewer should:

- Speak off topic with the subject, in the beginning of the interview, about something unrelated to the investigation. The interviewer should establish a rapport by finding an endearing quality in the subject that can be complimented.

- Share some information, to the extent possible, on the scope of the inquiry with the subject so that they feel they are part of the investigation—not just someone being interrogated. After stating that the subject's help is needed, the investigator should ask the subject if they are willing to assist.

- Ask the subject if there is any reason why the time, location, confidentiality, or other factors of the interview may not be conducive to a successful interview.

- Avoid interrupting, as a good interview involves careful listening. The investigator should not challenge conflicting information until the subject has completed telling the particulars of an event. Then the investigator may question discrepancies from other accounts of the events.

- Avoid being accusatory. If questioning a different version of the events, the investigator might say, "Wow, I am glad you were able to identify the precise time of the shooting; someone else I spoke to told me it was early, but your version sounds more reliable. Do you have any idea why someone else might say the shooting was earlier?"

Hypothetical Questions

If the subject of the interview is asking hypothetical questions, or trial balloon questions, then it may be a sign that they want to get information from the investigator to determine the consequences of what they may say next. It may also be a sign of guilt or suggest that they are ready to confess once they feel comfortable with the answers. An example would be a subject asking, "What would happen if I told you I knew where the money was?" or "If someone were to tell you where the money was, could they be charged in the crime?" If the subject of the interview asks these types of questions, the interviewer should maintain their composure, answer in the same tone and manner as before, and try to gently usher the subject toward feeling comfortable enough to confess what they know. Being accusatory or getting excited before securing the confession could make the subject reluctant to reveal their full knowledge.

Listening

Listening is the most important process in the interview. The subject has the information and the only way the investigator can retrieve it is to listen. The investigator should not interrupt the subject and must permit them to get out their full thoughts and statements. The investigator should provide the subject with full undivided attention. Taking telephone calls, interrupting the subject to take notes, or permitting distractions, will not provide the best results for the interviewer. An occasional nod of the head in affirmation is a good technique if done at the appropriate junctures to make the subject feel more comfortable.

Workplace Investigation Interviews

Many investigations originate from events that occurred in the workplace. When this happens, an investigator may be called in to conduct interviews at the job site. Investigators should be aware that if they discover a criminal act has been committed, the police agency of jurisdiction must be immediately notified and would supersede the investigator's own investigation. If the investigation is not of a criminal nature, then the investigator should choose a location for interviews on the employer's premises that would provide the least amount of workplace interruption and yield the most confidentiality for all subjects involved.

In workplace interviews, the range of subjects for interviews could include:

- An employee who is accused of misconduct
- Co-workers of the employee accused of misconduct
- Customers
- Visitors
- Vendors
- Supervisors
- Security personnel
- Other witnesses, as may be identified

The interviewer should prepare for the interview by learning as much background information as they can, which may include the subject's employment history, discipline history, history of theft, and breaches or other security concerns the employer may have had in the past that may or may not relate to the current investigation. Video evidence, if available, should be viewed and preserved to determine if there is any information that would assist the investigator in formulating a comprehensive understanding of historical information that may relate to the current investigation.

Canvassing

Canvassing is exploring every possible area for subjects who may have seen, heard, or otherwise been exposed to information involving the investigation. This process is challenging because it involves a great deal of time and resources. It may involve speaking to multiple persons to try to identify someone who may have relevant information. It also involves resourcefulness because the interviewer has to determine all persons who had access to a crime scene or scene of investigation, while utilizing multiple

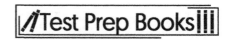

avenues of exploration such as the internet, motor vehicle records, camera footage, etc., to try to track down potential witnesses. The investigator is often faced with negative results, which can be discouraging.

Statements

Written Statements

Investigators need to support the information obtained during the interview in a written statement that should be signed by the person interviewed. If a notary is available, the signature should be notarized. The statement can be written for the subject to review and sign, after agreeing that it captures their statement accurately, or the subject can write it and sign it themselves. If the interview is video or audio recorded, then a signature is not necessary. But it is preferable if both can be obtained. The statement should include at a minimum the following information:

- Case information, including the identity of the investigator. It should also be noted if the interview was audio or video recorded.

- The date, time, and location of the interview

- Identification of the subject of the interview: name, address, contact information, and date of birth, if the subject wishes to provide it. It should be clarified in writing that consent was obtained for the interview and subsequent statement signature.

- Identify the relationship of the subject as it pertains to the investigation. For example, "employee where the incident occurred" or "spouse of the victim."

- Verify the particulars of the incident under investigation with the subject to include the date, time, location, weather, persons involved, and any other specific details that may be pertinent to the investigation with as much detail as possible for names, addresses, descriptions, other witnesses, etc.

- A countersignature of the signed statement by a witness to the interview, if possible. Both the subject and the witness should date their signatures. If available, a notary should validate the signatures.

- A confidential informant number. If the interview is of a confidential nature and the subject does not want to be officially on the record, for purposes of the report the investigator can assign a "CI" number, or confidential informant number, that will permit the investigator to keep the identity of the subject concealed until absolutely necessary for court proceedings, should the case proceed to that stage.

- Specific page numbering. Each page should be numbered to reflect where it stands in the statement as a whole, such as "1 of 3 pages" or "2 of 7 pages," etc.

Oral Statements

An oral statement comprises words spoken or heard that can be admissible in court. Private investigators, unlike police, do not have an obligation to read defendants the Miranda Warning and can collect oral statements that can be introduced in court proceedings, provided the following requirements are met:

- The investigator must support that the statement was made of the subject's own free will or was a spontaneous utterance and was not forced, coerced, or offered in exchange for any form of compensation.

- If there is a recording of the statement available, it must be identified and labeled, and should contain only the specific recording needed for the court. The recording should be audible without splices, interruptions, or missing segments, to be considered credible.

- When recording subjects there should not be "off the record" conversations that might cast doubt on the recorded portions of the interview.

- The tape as evidence should follow a chain of custody, which is documenting who had possession of the recording from the time it was made until the time it was produced for court.

- If additional copies are being made, the original should be safeguarded so that it can be produced for the court or law enforcement authorities, if needed, to authenticate the duplicate copy.

Narrative Statements

A narrative statement tells a story, depicting an event from before it began. It states the subject's relationship to the event, and then takes the interviewer or reader through to just before the event, then to the event, and finally to the event aftermath, while adding any other information along the way that may be pertinent. There should be no corrections in the statement.

- The statement should be identified with the date, time, location, interviewer, subject's name and contact information, names of any other witnesses in the room, and whether the statement was audio or video recorded.

- The statement should answer the "who, what, why, how, and when" of the event being investigated.

- If the person being interviewed does not speak or write English, then a certified translator should assist with the interview and translation of the statement.

Question and Answer Statements

The investigator should prepare for the interview, to obtain maximum results and to ensure they don't forget to ask anything pertinent. That means preparing a series of questions in advance to ensure comprehensive questioning conducted in a logical order. The opening questions should establish some background and identification information of the subject being interviewed, such as their name, contact information, and their relationship to the event under investigation. This establishes some basic facts about the person being interviewed, and the easy preliminary questions should set them at ease. The questioning should then progress into sequential questions into the event under investigation. As with a

narrative statement, in order for the question and answer statement to be recognized and accepted in court, it must:

- Be identified or labeled with the date, time, subject identity, interviewer identity, and any associated case or file number

- Be voluntary and not be forced, coerced, or given in exchange for compensation

- Be signed by the subject of the interview, so that it can't be easily refuted later

- Contain only factual information as believed to be true by the subject of the interview. Opinions or speculation are not valid or admissible.

Statement Format

The following are the elements of a good statement format. It should:

- Begin with an acknowledgement that it is provided voluntarily of the subject's free will. The subject of the interview should be identified at the beginning of the statement format, along with as much personal information as the subject feels comfortable providing, but no less than their name, address, contact information, and relationship to the crime scene or event under investigation.

- Identify the event that the subject is being interviewed about so subsequent readers can verify that the subject and interviewer were clear on the event being investigated.

- Provide an exact account of the event as described by the subject, in chronological order of what was witnessed, overheard, and/or observed. Anything indirectly related that they can recall that may not seem important to them or the investigator at the moment, but may become more important as the investigation progresses, should also be included.

- Close with the date, time, and signatures of the subject, investigator, and any witnesses present, in order to authenticate the statement at a later date.

Body Language

Just as important as spoken words during an interview are the unspoken body movements, facial expressions, posture, and nonverbal cues of the subject. They can show that a subject may be scared, nervous, or hiding something. It is important to observe and even record notes about nonverbal cues that may be valuable. The following are some of those cues:

- *Head position*: If the head is tilted and leaning forward it shows the subject has an interest in the investigation and is likely cooperative and truthful. If the head is tilted back it may mean the subject is trying to put some distance between the investigator and themselves or may be aggressive. A chin tilted down is generally associated with sorrow or remorse.

- *Eye contact*: Looking into the eyes of the investigator with momentary blinks is common. If the subject looks away, they may be lying about the question. If they look to the ceiling, they may be close to confession. The investigator should also note if the pupils are dilated, which might support active substance use that could affect the interview results.

- *Eyebrows*: If both raise with the subject's mouth open it could support genuine surprise to a question. Squeezed together they could support an angry or confused subject.

- *Hands*: Hands crossed with the subject leaning back is a defensive position. This would generally suggest that the subject will be uncooperative or could offer false information to throw the investigator off. If the subject's hands are covering their eyes, it suggests they may want to escape; hands over the mouth suggests they are trying to stop from talking.

- *Feet*: Fidgety feet support nervousness. Feet tucked under the body on a chair is defensive, suggesting the subject has something to hide. One foot forward and one foot back, or both feet in front and uncrossed, is generally associated with truthfulness.

Symptoms of Deception

Physiological Symptoms

While most individuals handle stress differently, the interview should be relatively stress free for any individual being earnest and truthful. In general, the more the subject is lying or intentionally withholding information, then the more stressed they will become. The interviewer should be aware of signs such as unusual perspiration, dizziness, or irritability. Some subjects may also have preexisting medical conditions that may affect their physiological state. The investigator is prohibited by law from asking the subject medically protected information but can ask if they need water, or anything from their purse or other area, prior to starting the interview.

The interview room should be well lit and well ventilated, and the interviewer should try to make the subject as comfortable as possible. With this understanding in mind, barring any preexisting medical conditions or comfort related issues, the subject should be physiologically stable throughout the interview unless they are the victim. If a subject is nervous, fidgety, exhibits tics or spasms, complains of headaches, etc., then an interviewer could conclude that stress from lying or withholding information might be the cause.

Verbal Symptoms

Below are some verbal cues that strongly suggest a subject of an interview or interrogation is lying. The subject:

- Gives inconsistent statements. They say things that don't make sense or provide confusing statements that contradict their earlier statements.

- Does not answer the question directly and defaults to another topic

- Repeatedly says, "I am telling the truth" or "to be truthful," or "to be honest"

- Overuses objections. The subject not only denies the accusations but also provides explanations.

- Attempts to distract the investigator from a line of questioning by complimenting the investigator's clothing, look, or mannerisms

- Leads the investigator on a trail well outside the scope of reality based upon what is being investigated in an effort to throw the investigator off the right trail

Below are some verbal cues that suggest that the subject is being truthful. The subject:

- Answers questions freely without hesitation and seems comfortable during the interview

- Offers more information than is being sought, which suggests they are trying to be as helpful as possible

Pathological Liars

Investigators may come across pathological liars during the course of their interviews. Pathological liars are experts at fabricating stories so detailed they seem vivid, and they present themselves so enthusiastically that most laypersons will readily believe the stories they tell. Investigators interviewing a pathological liar are generally met with superlative stories and grandiose accomplishments that almost sound too extraordinary to be true. Cross-referencing facts or other accounts of what the suspected pathological liar is reporting should provide some insight into whether any suspicion of their behavior is warranted. Pathological liars typically are defensive when confronted about lying, tell lies often, and can be so convincing that they believe the lies themselves.

Methods of Obtaining Confessions

Truthfulness
A suspect or the target of an investigation generally has no motivation to readily cooperate with an investigator. An investigator may employ lawful tactics to provide misleading information to gauge the subject's response. For example, an investigator investigating a burglary can tell a suspect that he was identified by a witness at the scene even if no such witness exists. If the suspect were innocent, then the natural response would be, "That is impossible—I was nowhere near that location." If the suspect is guilty, that tactic might elicit a confession or admission. An investigator cannot, however, present false direct evidence such as forged documents, manipulated photos, false test results, etc. The courts recognize that the investigator can use deceptive tactics to verify the validity of a subject's response but cannot outright manipulate evidence, data, or results as direct evidence.

Threats
On occasion subjects and targets of investigation have attempted to refute their previous statements to investigators, especially when the investigation rises to the level of a court of law. This is precisely why the interviews should be recorded, when possible, with the subject's consent. When not possible, the next best thing is to have the individual sign a statement acknowledging that they provided the statement of their own free will and were not coerced or threatened. In the past, cases have been thrown out of court or ruled inadmissible based upon threats or coercion during the interview.

Investigators must be very cognizant to avoid the appearance of threat to the subject's person or family; any threats related to reporting the subject, a friend, or family member to immigration; reporting them to another jurisdiction for something unrelated to the investigation; threatening the subject with separation from children, arrest, or deportation of other family members; or anything that would give the appearance that the subject did not provide the information of their own free will.

Promises and False Promises
During the course of interview, as an investigator learns more about the subject, it is not uncommon for the subject to reveal a need they may have. The needs may vary from police protection, anonymity, a referral to social services, small change for food or coffee, a letter of cooperation to a court or

jurisdiction, and the like. If the request is earnest and within the capacity of the investigator to grant, the investigator may accommodate it without fear of the statement becoming inadmissible. The subject should be accommodated if the investigator believes it is in the best interest of the subject, and the courts, and is lawful. Granting a request is not done to elicit the kind of statement the investigator is seeking. Statements are inadmissible when they are "quid pro quo," where the investigator made only a promise of fulfilling a request in exchange for a statement, or the promise was false because it was never within the investigator's power to fulfill. For example, an investigator can ask for leniency for a subject but never guarantee it. If a statement is elicited under the promise of leniency, it is inadmissible.

Confidence

An investigator must be composed, prepared, and exuding confidence even if their case is weak, or many facts are still unknown. If the subject of the interview or target of the investigation senses a nervous, unprepared, or unskilled investigator, they will not be as compelled to speak. Preparation is an important part of an investigator becoming confident for the interview. Doing research prior to the interview, outlining questions beforehand, and developing a strategy and flow will only help build the investigator's confidence before the interview.

There are reasons why some investigators are better than others, and it has to do with preparation, the employment of the interview tactics described in this material, and a strong persistence to get to the facts and truth. The investigator's confidence should not come across as demeaning or condescending but rather as authoritative in a relentless pursuit of the truth.

Taking control of the interview, the investigator can set a tone that is friendly or intimidating, depending upon what strategy they are trying to achieve. The goal is to evaluate the subject or suspect and extract the information they may have. Selecting the most appropriate strategy, predicting a subject's reactions, anticipating those reactions, and adjusting follow-up questions accordingly, will all achieve the best results.

Nonverbal tone is important as well and if the investigator wants to convey a tone of seriousness, they will be formal and methodical, which may intimidate the subject into cooperation. If the investigator wants to convey a tone of comfort to encourage the subject to loosen up and drop their guard, then the investigator may begin with some light conversation and overemphasize a friendly relationship at the start of the interview.

Legal Tactics

Investigators are not required to read a suspect or subject of an interview the Miranda Warning before questioning. This protocol is only lawful for law enforcement officers in their area of jurisdiction. The following are some examples of far-reaching interview tactics that are within the confines of the law:

- While the investigator can't fabricate evidence to present to a subject to get them to confess, they can present a strong hunch to make the subject feel that the investigator knows more than they really do. An example would be that of an investigator who believes a suspect was at the crime scene, even though no witnesses saw them, and who says to the suspect, "Multiple witnesses saw you there; how do you respond to that?"

- If it will help the interview, the investigator should trivialize things the suspect says, to make the suspect think the situation isn't as serious as it really is; the investigator does not want to stop the suspect from possibly confessing. An example would be a suspect that is charged with sexual assault who tells the investigator he was smoking narcotics prior to meeting a woman. If the

investigator stops the suspect when he discusses the drug use, advising him that it is illegal, then the suspect might not want to discuss the sexual assault for fear he will be judged like he was for the narcotic use. If, on the other hand, the investigator says in response, "We have all done drugs at one time or another, this is no big deal, go on with the story," it would be recognized as a lawful tactic on the part of the investigator to exact the rest of the story.

- The investigator should provide strong motivation for the suspect to confess, such as, if the subject gets it off their chest they will feel better, or if they reveal the circumstances now it will look better than if a DNA test or another test proves they were involved later on.

Special Tactics

The investigator must weigh the balance between the employment of deception and how the court will view the tactics used to obtain a confession. Courts don't always rule in finite terms or interpretations. Good judgment on how far to proceed when interviewing—and what tactics to use—should be exercised in considering what may seem fair and reasonable to an impartial judge or jury if the investigation should progress to that phase.

Informants

Informants provide information to investigators for a variety of reasons. In most cases, the informant wants consideration in their own criminal proceeding; in other cases, they are paid a small fee; or in yet other cases, they are helpful to avoid further investigation into their own activities. Sometimes they have a desire to see justice, but regardless of motive, if they are classified as an informant, then they have a strong desire to keep their identity secret. The investigator should firmly protect that identity in order to maintain trust between the investigator and the informant, which will protect the safety of the informant and, it is hoped, lead to gathering additional information in the future from that informant. When dealing with informants, an investigator should follow these guidelines:

- Recognize that the informant is providing information in exchange for something. The investigator must consider the value of what the informant might provide, along with what cost it might bear in credibility to provide what the informant wants.

- Consider the informant's history of verifiable information; the more accurate they have been in the past should suggest how reliable they will be in the current investigation.

- Never write the informant's name on a piece of paper or document that others might view. Most investigators assign a special coding or "CI" number, so if the document is reviewed by another party then the identity of the informant will remain anonymous until needed to be revealed to a judge or pursuant to a court proceeding.

- Never ask the informant to violate the law or report their involvement in crimes. It should be made clear that the investigator has an obligation to report crimes committed or present hearsay evidence if called to testify in a court of law.

- Treat informants with respect and not make promises that will damage credibility.

- *Informant* is sometimes viewed as a derogatory term, but good, ordinary, citizens become informants because they want to assist the police or private investigations. They don't want to be stigmatized, however, and so prefer to keep their identity anonymous.

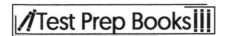

Miranda Warning Ruling

In 1966, a 23-year-old man with the last name of Miranda was arrested as a suspect in a sexual assault. He was poor, uneducated, and without access to an attorney. After two hours of intense police questioning, he confessed to the crime. During the subsequent court proceedings, the Supreme Court ruled that the police should have let the suspect know his Fourth Amendment rights before they questioned him and should have told him that he had the right to remain silent, among other rights.

After the Miranda vs. Arizona ruling, all police jurisdictions were required to read a suspect their rights before questioning. The only exception is the public safety exemption that says a police officer can question a suspect without reading the Miranda Warning if there is imminent danger to public safety, such as finding a suspect who planted a bomb and asking them where it is if it has not yet been found. Again, this ruling only applies to sworn law enforcement officers acting in an official capacity and not to private investigators. Police must inform the suspect that:

- They have the right to remain silent.

- Anything they say can be used in court against them.

- They have a right to an attorney before questioning.

- If they are poor and can't afford an attorney, the court can appoint one for them if they desire.

- They have the right to an attorney whose services will be free of charge.

- Anything said of the subject's free will without questioning that is heard by that law enforcement officer can be admitted into court.

The Fifth Amendment

The Fifth Amendment essentially states that in a grand jury proceeding, if a witness is called to testify, they may invoke their constitutional right not to incriminate themselves and remain silent. The court can, however, draw inferences from this and still find a defendant guilty based upon their silence and other evidence produced during the proceedings. A private investigator cannot force a subject to speak or incriminate themselves, and all information gathered must be voluntary from the subject. If called to a grand jury or criminal proceeding involving a felony, a private investigator can also invoke their right to remain silent if they feel something they say may incriminate themselves.

Intensity of Review and Encouragement

The speed and intensity of interviews can vary greatly based upon the subject's demeanor and reaction. Subjects who are nervous and willing to talk but appear afraid may need soft encouragement to open up, and other subjects who are stoic or rigid may require loud and fast questioning to try to rattle them into speaking. Therefore, the intensity of the interview should increase or decrease depending upon the subject and the type of information the investigator is trying to obtain.

For example, the lowest levels of intensity should be for reviewing general details and cursory information; the mid-level intensity should be reserved for obtaining specific details and information; and the highest levels of intensity used when confronting a subject with specific facts they may not be

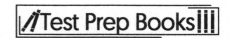

able to counter with a plausible explanation, which in turn might compel them to confess or incriminate themselves as they try to explain further.

Polygraph

Polygraph exams, commonly referred to as *lie detector tests*, are inadmissible in a court of law. They can be part of an employment exam or used to suggest innocence or guilt outside a court of law but must have the subject's consent to be administered. This is generally a useful tool to shift the onus of responsibility on a subject, to try to help support their innocence if they are claiming innocence. The premise behind the polygraph exam is that if a subject is lying they will be stressed during the questioning and will display indicators of stress that the equipment can measure. Polygraph exams are proven to be 100 percent reliable, which is why they can't be admitted into criminal proceedings.

Restrictions in Workplace Investigations

Many federal job applicants, such as those applying for employment in the Drug Enforcement Agency, for example, are subject to polygraph exams as a condition of employment. Other nonfederal employees must provide consent to participate in a polygraph exam and may do so voluntarily to prove their credibility or innocence. Whether or not they can be terminated, if they refuse to participate in a workplace related polygraph exam, would have to be decided by their employment agreement, other facts in the case being investigated, and the employer in consultation with their legal division or outside counsel. This is not something generally within the scope of an investigator and is related to the employer and the employee agreement.

Documentary Evidence

Documentary evidence is evidence that takes document or paper form that can be used to prove a fact in court. It is important for an investigator to help support their fact finding by reviewing documents, public records, and other physical sources of evidence. All of the following records are deemed credible and can be used by an investigator in the course of an investigation, and if needed can be presented in a court of law:

- *Government records*: Copies of license verifications, driving records, databases, publicly disclosed court proceeding records, and anything else published by any government or municipality is a solid source of information.

- *Legal documents*: Most legal proceedings are public record and readily available at no charge or in some cases are available to any requestor for a nominal fee.

- *Logs or logbooks and reports*: Employment records, work schedules, and work-related documents can be considered documentary evidence if obtained lawfully and can be authenticated by the employer.

- *Public education records*: These are open-source documents as they may be available. In order to get educational transcripts, a subject is generally required to sign a release.

Invasion of Privacy

When conducting investigations, the investigator should consider violations of individuals' privacy. While the interpretation of what is a normal and reasonable expectation of privacy is generally decided according to arguments in a court of law, the following four criteria are each considered as standards when rendering those decisions:

- *Intrusion of solitude*: Many times, the interpretation of what is considered an invasion of solitude is decided by a court or jury. Examples of invasion are an investigator recording someone on the phone without their knowledge and while not being a party to the call; video recording a subject without their knowledge in a nonpublic place; and peering into a subject's house through windows or by use of high-powered magnifying lenses. These examples go beyond public viewing, and the subject would have a reasonable expectation of privacy under such circumstances.

- *Use of someone's name or likeness*: This is simply pretending to be someone else or misrepresenting oneself as someone who may have similar characteristics.

- *The public disclosure of a private fact*: The investigator cannot expose medically protected information, records, facts obtained during an investigation, or knowledge that the general public would not be able to obtain through open sources or readily available public records.

- *Shedding false light*: Shedding false light is alluding to or stating that someone did something when in fact it is not proven. To meet the criteria for false light, the lie generally needs to be published, reckless, portray the person offended in a false light, and be considered embarrassing for the subject.

To reiterate, any person can bring forth a lawsuit or claim involving the invasion of privacy; the burden of proof is upon them. However, staying within the guidelines of what is generally accepted as reasonable privacy and keeping abreast of governing legislation will help the investigator avoid any legal challenges to the lawfulness of their tactics.

Conducting Research

When commencing an investigation, it is imperative to conduct research, collecting open-source intelligence, to understand the history of the subject of the interview as well as historical facts related to the investigation. This intelligence should help define the line of questioning with subjects. Investigators should:

- Decide where to look: An investigator should determine what type of intelligence might be of value and select the sources. For example, the investigator may want to see any arrest histories of a subject, to look for patterns, check news articles about them, or review their accessible social media profiles.

- Collect data: An investigator must actually find the data and assemble it in useful order.

- Interpret data: In this step, an investigator analyzes data to determine its relationship to the investigation.

- Present data: In order to prove the findings of the investigation, the investigator may be required to present the findings to a client, a court of law, or to use it to confront a subject of an interview to illustrate the known acts they may be disputing.

When collecting information, the subject's right to privacy must not be violated. The investigator should check and understand state laws and guidelines as they relate to privacy rights. Information must be obtained through legitimate methods and be able to ethically stand up in court.

Electronically Sourcing Information and the Use of Search Engines

The advent of the internet has made the investigator's job much easier. Limitless information is available literally at the fingertips of the investigator; therefore, the use of this method has gained tremendous popularity. Electronic evidence can also be found in emails, databases, computer files, and any electronic record.

- There are many search engines available to gather open-source information on the web. Google is currently the most widely used search engine in the world, followed by Bing, Yahoo!, and Ask.com.

- Checking social media profiles for subjects of interviews is lawful if they can be found on the internet freely without decoding passwords or other protection devices and can provide some personal details about the subject.

- Many arrest records are now public knowledge and can be located open source on the web.

- When searching on the web, entering a word or words in quotations should only reveal findings with those words or phrases, which will help refine the search.

- Using words such as "and," "or," or "not" should help narrow down the search when sourcing information on commonly used names or terms.

There are several ways for an investigator to find personal information about a subject. Some proprietary search databases, such as Lexis Nexis, used by private investigators to search for persons, require a subscription and fee. Most search engines, such as Google, Bing, and Yahoo!, do permit a free search through local white pages that generally reveal some basic information such as name and town, name and address, or name and number, and then try to sell additional information such as email addresses, other persons living at the residence, length of residence, etc. The searcher will also be inundated with other vendors that can provide extensive reports that expand to criminal histories, known associates, and other public records for varying fees. Some of these vendors' services are reasonable and will yield results for investigators that are beneficial to the investigation.

The Internet

The internet has many advantages as a research tool. Its accessibility, speed, and availability of information is truly limitless as new data is added as it happens. It permits precise search focus and the ability to quickly verify facts, but it does have some disadvantages.

Disadvantages:

- When searching their own media presence, an individual may be able to determine that someone else (an investigator, for instance) searched it with tracking software.

- When searching for commonly used names, the investigator may be overwhelmed with incorrect responses.

- Information, while readily available, sometimes lacks authenticity.

- The information obtained can sometimes be subjective, meaning it comes with an opinion, as opposed to objective data that permit the document, statement, or fact, to speak on its own merit.

- Some websites employ a tracking program that permits them to see who visited their site, which may identify an investigator's search.

Sources of Information

Physical Sources
Physical sources cannot be found on the internet but instead are tangible records that may be uncovered during Internet searches. Physical sources can be found at the local, state, and federal level. Physical sources can be used as documentary evidence in court procedures. They may include original copies of items such as: birth records, marriage records, divorce records, business records, legal documents, documents published by the government, scientific documents, etc.

Federal Agencies
With over 400 current federal agencies, there is no shortage of publicly available government information. The federal government operates under transparency and is obligated where warranted to continually release public records from its various agencies. There are too many agencies to list, but contacting agencies will yield the investigator the following types of documents (note that this is not an inclusive list):

- Company, bids, awards, company principals, and business addresses of those doing business with the government
- Sales figures, business size, and dollar amounts of transactions
- Patents, trademarks, federal lawsuits, and actions
- Military and educational records, discipline records, certifications, and awards
- Annual reports, date on business structures, and ownership

Under the *Freedom of Information Act*, an investigator can request any other internal agency document, which may be released barring any time limit on its release or confidentiality restriction due to the classification of the document.

State Government Sources
To maintain transparency, many states disclose that applications for licenses, permits, and other certifications are part of public records. In addition, tax information, marriage and birth records, along with other state recognized documents, are all part of public record. Agencies' titles and records available vary from state to state, and what follows is a non-inclusive list of some of the public documents that may be readily available to investigators:

- Court records for anything that was presented in state court
- Birth certificates, marriage certificates, death records, etc.
- Motor vehicle operation records
- Licensing agencies
- Regulatory agencies
- Criminal dispositions

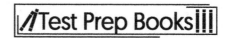

- Fines, sanctions, liens
- Tax information
- Any other state administered record

Local Government Sources

On a county or town level, the following types of documents may be available as a matter of public record:

- Real estate related information including liens, tax information, record or sale, owner of deed, blueprints, permits, etc.
- County court records
- County agencies reports and records
- Publicly available voter registration information
- County licensing agencies and permits

With the subject's written consent, the investigator can get access to educational records, human resource information, or even release of medical information from local sources.

Physical Research for Pre-Employment Investigations

In order to conduct a pre-employment investigation, the investigator must have the candidate's written consent, and the search is limited to those items that the candidate consented to. For example, if they consented to educational records only, then the investigator cannot lawfully search privacy protected medical records. If the consent form authorizes the release of medical records and the subject consents in writing, then it is permissible. Not all employers and agencies respond to written requests, but if the investigator can deliver a signed consent form and identify the purpose of the inquiry, with a little persistence the investigator should be able to obtain the documents that the candidate permitted to be released. Some examples of these document types include:

- A credit report maintained by Trans Union, Experian, or Equifax, which are credit reporting vendors, can be checked if consented to by the job candidate, especially if they are being considered for a position of trust.

- Certified copies of education records can be obtained from an educational institution, which can be forwarded to the investigator for verification, or the investigator can verify copies provided by the applicant with the institution.

- A criminal history search can be conducted by the investigator or by an independent vendor based upon known addresses provided by the applicant. In some cases, with consent, a fingerprint check can be conducted against state or federal databases.

- An employment history check can be conducted by calling references provided by the candidate.

- Military records can be verified against what the candidate provided to verify their discharge status, but the investigator will need their consent, name, social security number, and service dates.

- Many employers now also conduct a search of the candidate's social media profile to determine if they display substance abuse, racial and sexual deviation, cruelty to animals, etc.

- A substance test may also be a condition of employee or personal reference verification, which the private investigator may be involved in.

Access to Confidential Data

Not only do privacy restrictions vary from federal, state, and local levels, but when challenged they are also left up to interpretation of the court of jurisdiction in which they are challenged. It is for this reason that the private investigator must be familiar with the rules governing their licensing in the state, as well as the many federal, state, and local guidelines that govern privacy. As a rule, private investigators have more liberty and access to information if working lawfully at the request of a client but should be careful not to cross over those boundaries that govern the invasion of privacy. Any information that is publicly available is not governed by those restrictions, and with consent, the investigator can pursue any documents related to the type of consent the candidate provided.

The Federal Freedom of Information Act

This act permits transparency in government and permits individuals the right to request federal records and documents that the agency must produce upon request. There are certain restrictions to this, such as classified information that could place persons in danger. Under amendments, the Freedom of Information Act has extended to requests for government information on the state and local level. Private companies are not subject to provisions of the Freedom of Information Act.

Legislative Acts

The federal government has passed the following legislation that relates to access to public records, which the investigator should be aware of:

- Omnibus and Crime Control Bill of 1968: protects crime witnesses

- The Fair Credit Reporting Act of 1970: ensures fair and accurate credit reporting to agencies and individuals

- The Privacy Act of 1974: involves the protection or personal records

- The Financial Privacy Act of 1978: protects confidentiality of financial records

- The Privacy Protection Act of 1980: provides an individual a reasonable expectation of privacy

- The Fair Financial Information Practices Act of 1981: provides protection against fraudulent financial reporting for individuals

- The Privacy of Electronic Fund Transfers Act of 1981: provides confidentiality of electronic transfers

- Freedom of Information Act: requires each agency to provide to the public information on the agency's organization, locations, general course, and method

Fairness in Collection of Information

Investigators must follow certain guidelines as they relate to the pursuit and collection of personal data. The following requirements should be followed:

- A subject should provide consent for financial records, medically protected information, and other information that may fall under an invasion of privacy without such consent.

- Files with personal data should be locked or password protected as not to be accessed by others.

- The subject of the inquiry should be permitted to review the information obtained to verify its accuracy.

- If being viewed by others, sensitive information such as social security numbers or bank account numbers should be cleansed to ensure they are not copied on documents unless needed for court production.

Practice Questions

1. When conducting interviews of subjects who are not the target of the investigation, which of the following should be considered first?
   a. The investigator should try to get as much information from the subject "off the record" before the interview
   b. The investigator should introduce themselves and try to build a rapport before starting the interview
   c. The investigator should find a location that will make the subject feel uncomfortable and compelled to speak
   d. The investigator should interview the target first and then other witnesses

2. After taking a written statement from a subject, the statement should be:
   a. Signed by the witness to the interview and the investigator
   b. Signed by the witness to the interview and subject of the interview, and notarized if possible
   c. Signed by the subject of the interview unless the interview was audio or video recorded
   d. Signed by the investigator and notarized if possible

3. Which of the following would likely be admissible in court?
   a. A confession obtained from a suspect after being misled during an interview
   b. A confession obtained from a subject after being threatened with deportation of a friend
   c. A true confession obtained from a subject after being threatened with violence but not hurt
   d. None of the following would be admissible in court

4. Which of the following is the BEST way for an interviewer to compose themselves during an interview when confronted with troubling information or heinous activity?
   a. When the subject reveals this information, the investigator should react with shock and emotion to let the subject know this is problematic.
   b. They should maintain their composure during the interview so as to not impact the subject's responses.
   c. They should react as they normally would, to keep the interview as real as possible.
   d. They should confront the subject immediately on any troubling or heinous information.

5. One of the MOST important qualities of all good interviewing involves which of the following?
   a. Aggressive interview tactics
   b. Comprehensive note taking
   c. Good listening
   d. A hint of deception, which is considered lawful

6. When the subject of an interview begins to ask hypothetical questions it is generally a sign that:
   a. They can't understand the questioning and they require a simple breakdown of questions.
   b. They may be the target of an investigation.
   c. They may have something to hide and may be ready to confess.
   d. They want to check the investigator's answers to determine who the suspect may be.

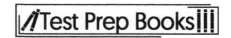

7. In reference to workplace interviews and investigations which of the following is TRUE?

    a. In order to conduct a background check on a candidate, written consent is required.

    b. In order to conduct a background check on a candidate, written consent is not required if ordered by the employer.

    c. A background check on an employee can be conducted only if consented to by the employer as part of a criminal investigation.

    d. Only local laws and guidelines will determine if background checks of employees are permitted.

8. Which is MOST TRUE about Miranda Warnings?

    a. An investigator must read all suspects their Miranda Warnings before questioning.

    b. An investigator must read all suspects *and* interview subjects their Miranda Warnings before questioning in order for information obtained to be admissible in court.

    c. An investigator does not have to read a suspect their Miranda Warnings before questioning, but any information obtained will not be admissible in court.

    d. Miranda Warnings are only required to be read by police officers having jurisdiction.

9. According to the material which is the BEST answer to describe what a narrative statement should answer?

    a. The "who, what and why, when and how" of an investigation

    b. Who the possible suspects are

    c. How the investigator came to the conclusion

    d. Fundamental questions of the investigator

10. According to the study material on body language, if a subject has their chin tilted down it generally means what?

    a. They are trying to remain distant and putting some distance between the interviewer and them.

    b. They are cooperative and comfortable to speak.

    c. They are sorrowful and remorseful.

    d. They will be uncooperative.

11. The Fifth Amendment involves what?

    a. The right to a reasonable expectation of privacy

    b. The right against illegal search and seizure

    c. The right against self-incrimination

    d. The right to freedom of speech

12. Which of the following is legally permitted for an investigator to obtain from open sources?

    a. Medical records

    b. Social media profiles

    c. Credit information

    d. None of the following are permissible for an investigator to get without the subject's consent.

13. As it relates to false promises, when questioning subjects, which of the following is the MOST improper and can jeopardize a statement or witness account?
    a. Providing a letter of cooperation for the subject to a court, asking for leniency for the subject
    b. Providing a referral to social services for the subject, based upon their request during the interview
    c. Obtaining the statement in exchange for assistance in an unrelated matter
    d. All of the answers are improper and can jeopardize a statement or witness account.

14. Which of the following BEST describes a leading question for an investigator investigating a death?
    a. "Did you kill Mary?"
    b. "Who killed Mary?"
    c. "Why would you kill Mary?"
    d. "I know you killed Mary, didn't you?"

15. In the legality of privacy standards, the court will consider four criteria. Intrusion of solitude, using someone's name or likeness, public disclosure of a private fact, and shedding false light. Which of the following BEST describes false light?
    a. Recording someone without their permission
    b. Pretending to be someone else
    c. Exposing medically protected or credit related information
    d. Alluding or stating someone did something when in fact they did not

Answer Explanations

1. B: The investigator should try to make the subject as comfortable as possible to disarm them and make them feel comfortable enough to speak. There is no such thing as "off the record," as everything stated to a private investigator should be on the record. As far as a location, it should make witnesses comfortable so they want to speak to the investigator and the investigator should try when possible to interview the target of an investigation last, so that there is information from witnesses to confront the target with.

2. B: In order to authenticate the statement, it needs to be signed by the subject of the interview so they can confirm it represents their statement, and by any witnesses. When possible, a notary can validate signatures, which can't be refuted at a later date. Choice A would defeat the purpose of the subject verifying their statement. For Choice C, even if the interview is recorded, it wouldn't confirm that the statement being presented at a later date is the one being viewed in the video. Choice D also doesn't confirm that the subject agrees with the statement so it is useless.

3. A: It is lawful to mislead a subject during questioning as long as the interviewer doesn't tamper or create factual evidence. Choices B and C are incorrect because an interviewer can't threaten a subject.

4. B: The investigator must maintain their composure, otherwise the subject may react differently if they realize they are being judged by the investigator. Choice A would defeat that purpose and stop the subject from revealing more information, Choice C is arbitrary and may elicit the wrong reaction, and Choice D would essentially stop the interview and prevent the investigator from getting additional information from the subject.

5. C: Good listening is the cornerstone of good interviewing. In Choice A, aggressive tactics are usually reserved for targets of the investigation and are not universal to all investigations. In Choice B, note taking when appropriate is recommended but not so comprehensive as to make the subject feel the investigator is not listening, looking the subject in the eye, and personalizing the interview. For Choice D, deception, while a useful interview technique, is not to be applied universally and is generally reserved for obtaining a confession.

6. C: If a subject is asking hypothetical questions, then they are trying to gain some assurance or answers to determine just how much trouble they may be in or what the investigator's response would be. Choice A is incorrect because if the subject can't understand the investigator's question, then they will just ask for it to be restated. For Choice B, it may not be just the target of the investigation that may ask hypothetical questions. It may also be an accomplice or accomplice unknown to the investigator at the time of the interview. Choice D is incorrect because the subject themselves may be the suspect so they don't really need to know.

7. A: With a person's consent, the background check can be conducted. Choice B is incorrect because while the employer may in fact order the background check, it must be accompanied by the employee's consent, which is generally a condition of employment. Choice C is incorrect because if it is part of a criminal investigation, then it will be a law enforcement agency seeking the documents, and they will not need anyone's consent if they have a subpoena. Choice D is incorrect because while local laws and guidelines may govern background checks, they are not the only determination, and the consent by the subject as stated in Choice A would override local laws.

8. D: Miranda Warnings only pertain to sworn law enforcement officers in the course of their duties within the jurisdiction they are sworn in. Private investigators do not have to adhere to the same standard, so all other answers are incorrect.

9. A: A narrative statement should answer the "who, what, why, when and how" of an investigation. Choice *B* is incorrect because a statement can still be narrative without any suspects being identified. Choice *C* is incorrect because the conclusion is just one component of the narrative statement. Choice *D* may be contained in a narrative statement because the statement may answer all the investigator's questions, but not in a narrative statement per se, so it is not the best answer.

10. C: If the subject's chin is tilted down, it generally means they are remorseful and sorrowful and may be close to confession. Choice *A*, they may have the head tilted back. Choice *B*, being cooperative and comfortable, is often associated with the head tilted forward and leaning forward.

11. C: The Fifth Amendment involves the right to remain silent, therefore no suspect is required by law to speak and incriminate themselves. They may "take the Fifth," which invokes this constitutional right. Choices *A* and *B*, the right to a reasonable expectation of privacy and the right against illegal search and seizure refer to the Fourth Amendment.

12. B: Social media profiles are not permitted an expectation of privacy because the subject posted it on an open-source platform, such as the web, and should have no expectation of privacy. Medical records (Choice *A*) are HIPPA protected and credit information (Choice *C*) requires the subject's consent, therefore, Choice *D* would not be applicable.

13. C: The key word is *exchange*. During the course of interview, as the investigator learns more about the person being interviewed, it is not uncommon for the subject to reveal a need they may have. The needs may vary from police protection, to requesting to remain anonymous, perhaps a referral to social services, small change for food or coffee, or even a letter or cooperation to a court or jurisdiction. If the request is earnest and within the capabilities of the investigator, the investigator may accommodate the request without fear of the statement becoming inadmissible. The only way the statement would not be admissible is if it was a "quid pro quo" where the investigator only made promises in *exchange* for a statement or the promise was false and never within the scope of the investigator, understanding the they can ask for leniency for a subject but never guarantee it.

14. C: A leading question is a question that already makes an assumption in order to lead a suspect to believe that the investigator knows more than they do, and to lead the subject to an anticipated response. Choice *A* is incorrect because it is a general question, making no assumptions. Choice *B* is incorrect because it asks a simple open-ended question. Choice *D* is incorrect because it is an accusatory statement with an open-ended question.

15. D: Shedding false light is alluding or stating that someone did something when in fact it is not proven. In general, it needs to be published, reckless, portray the person offended in a false light, and be considered embarrassing for the subject. Choice *A* is intrusion of solitude. Choice *B* is using someone's name or likeness, and Choice *C* is public disclosure of a private fact.

Evidence Collection

A crime has occurred. From the moment dispatch receives the 911 call for police, fire, and rescue responders to arrive, the clock has started on a crucial chain of events. Every second counts. The first 48 hours are considered the "golden hours" in investigating and collecting evidence in any criminal case. While this is a job for law enforcement employees, private investigators should be knowledgeable about the evidence collection process and procedures as they may be called on to use similar skill sets for clients or provide evidence to a member of the police force in an ongoing investigation.

A 911 dispatch officer's initial goal is to collect as much detailed information (oral evidence) from the caller in order to answer some very basic but important questions. What is your emergency? Where is your emergency?

One may not think that this is part of the "evidence collection process," but it is, even before police and emergency medical services (EMS) arrive on the scene and begin to rope off the area with yellow and black "crime scene" tape.

There is no perfect crime. In every crime committed, there is a transfer of evidence. The first person to recognize these facts was Dr. Edmond Locard of Lyon, France. His theory, "Locard's Exchange Principle," is the foundational principle of criminal forensic studies to this day. From Dr. Locard, information about the transfer of physical evidence when a person comes in contact with another person or place or surface area became widely known.

Although many police officers don't relish the assignment of "protecting the crime scene" and may feel that this assignment is menial, in reality it's one of the most important assignments on a scene. The investigator will then begin to carry out what is known as the Seven S's of Crime Scene Investigation (CSI), which will be covered later.

The police enforce the laws and investigate crime, and the prosecutor prosecutes those crimes. However, this occurs only after highly trained law enforcement, legal, and scientific professionals have effectively done their jobs – professional men and women who labor daily and diligently in the field of criminal justice and who are employed with titles such as:

- CSI team leader
- Crime scene investigator
- Photographer and photographic log recorder
- Sketch prep technician
- Evidence recorder/evidence recovery personnel
- Specialist
- Evidence technician
- Criminalist
- Coroner or medical examiner
- Scientist in: forensics, accounting, computers
- Evidence custodian
- Property officer
- Latent print examiner
- Detective
- Police officer

No one member of the team is more important than the other. Each team member plays a crucial role in the gathering and processing of evidence.

So, what is *evidence*?

Evidence is the available body of facts or information indicating or tending to prove whether a belief or theory is true or valid. There are two types of evidence that can be used during court proceedings: direct and circumstantial.

Here are some examples of evidence:

- Oral argument or oral evidence (testimony)
- Presentation of documents and documentation review
- Written records, recorded audio records
- Electronic (computer forensics, cell phones, etc.)
- Firearm evidence
- Latent fingerprints
- Blood stains
- Seminal stains
- Hair analysis
- Glass
- Paint
- Fibers and threads
- Tool marks
- Controlled substance and medicinal preparations
- Flammable liquids

The Evidence-Gathering Team

The *CSI team leader* (usually a high-ranking law enforcement officer) is responsible for the thorough, precise, and efficient legal collection and processing of all the evidence left at the scene and elsewhere to solve a crime. This person:

- Is the agent-in-charge of the crime scene and will lead the "preliminary walk-through" of the scene.

- Is in command and responsible for the safety and security of all people on the scene

- Must see to it that all protocols are followed and strictly adhered to – with no exceptions – and protect the onsite team from blood products or other biohazard materials that may be harmful to the health of those assigned to the crime scene.

- Dictates assignments to the team

- Must establish a secure offsite command post to be certain there is a free flow of relevant information between the evidence gatherers and the detectives on the scene

- Is required to liaison and coordinate with all other law enforcement (local, state, and federal) and labor personnel to maintain a spirit of cross-departmental cooperation

- Must also see to it that the needed tools, equipment, and supplies are ready and available for his or her staff to complete the tasks at hand in a timely and effective manner

- Must give the orders to establish a secure perimeter and designate an officer to log everyone coming in and out of the scene. (Controlling access to the scene is crucial.)

- Continuously assesses the progress of the team

- Upon conclusion of these stated duties, gives orders to tear down the scene and to perform a final inventory of the evidence

The *crime scene investigator* is one of many important parts of the evidence-gathering process at the crime scene. If any of the personnel in the criminal justice system listed previously fails to do a job to his or her fullest abilities, the entire prosecution of the case could be ruined, and justice may not be served, perhaps allowing the guilty to go free or the innocent to be wrongly convicted.

The crime scene investigator's role is to help document, reconstruct, and collect evidence from the crime scene and aid in the process of finding the facts regarding the person or persons who committed the crime through the gathering and scientific analysis of the evidence.

This process must be a careful and deliberate one; it requires patience and persistence combined with an unyielding adherence and respect for the spirit and letter of the law. In that way, justice is given the best odds at ultimately prevailing.

The collection of the evidence must be completed with the utmost care. A good CSI investigator adheres to an intense attention to detail. It's also important to note that crime scene investigation is not as glamorous as television shows would lead one to believe.

In all investigations, evidence gathering must be conducted in an objective and thorough manner. The evidence gathered must be relevant to the case. Work must be timely and accurate, and it must be conducted by a person who is neutral, objective, and non-judgmental in his or her attitude toward the crime scene, the (alleged) perpetrators, and victims. The evidence must be permitted to "speak for itself." The evidence must substantiate any intuitions and guide the investigator, rather than the investigator driving or pushing the evidence. Bias and/or prejudice can only serve to taint the evidence and its collection.

A skilled evidence gatherer will work to answer the questions of who, what, where, when, why, and how the crime took place. Each question is relevant and deserves an answer.

The forensic investigator will begin the evidence-gathering process by conducting an initial walk-through of the scene.

This initial canvass of the crime scene is to simply locate the evidence so that it can be attended to in order of importance. Time is crucial. Investigators must work diligently, but not sloppily, since many forms of evidence can degrade with time. Some evidence, such as foot or shoe prints, is delicate in nature and can be ruined easily if trampled on or over. The investigator must wear protective footwear to avoid tainting or damaging any evidence when entering the crime scene.

Upon carefully entering the crime scene, the investigator must begin to establish a written log. That log must have a case number on it, since every case must have a number.

Attention to detail and writing skills are crucial to this line of work. The investigator must have a keen eye or a "sixth sense," which one develops from training and experience in the field for what may or may not be relevant.

Gathering Evidence

When gathering evidence, investigators should always use the proper equipment to accomplish their onsite tasks. The items in the following list are some of those that are considered standard and are housed in the investigator's "kit":

- Cotton swabs
- Latex or nitrate gloves
- Tweezers
- Forceps
- Paper bags
- Plastic bags
- Surgical scalpel
- Cardboard boxes
- Thermometer
- A large bucket with a locking lid to store liquids

Direct evidence is first-hand knowledge, first-person observations, eyewitness accounts or, for example, a source of evidence that is seen increasingly in today's news, such as video footage from police body or dashboard cameras. The camera records what the field of vision observes.

If a witness says, "Yes, officer, I saw the man who pulled the trigger — he was Caucasian, 5'4" with black hair and glasses. He had on blue jeans with a white T-shirt and had on a New York Yankees baseball cap." This is direct evidence.

Circumstantial evidence is indirect evidence that can be used to infer a fact.

For example, when a man goes to bed at night, before turning in, he might look out of the bedroom window and see the light from the moon illuminating the front yard and that there is no snow on the ground. However, when he wakes up in the morning, he sees the ground is covered in a fresh, new blanket of snow. From that fact, it can be inferred that it snowed overnight. This is very good circumstantial evidence – evidence that isn't seen, but that follows a logical pattern.

Although direct evidence carries more weight in the courtroom with a jury, circumstantial evidence gathered at a crime scene may provide a significant causal link between the crime scene and a suspect. People have been convicted and sentenced to prison based solely on circumstantial evidence.

Trace evidence to a CSI investigator is just as crucial to recognize and collect as any other form of evidence.

Every time two people come in contact with one another — or a person comes in contact with a place or thing, a physical transfer of trace evidence occurs. This is why it is so important to wash one's hands after shaking someone's hand, since this simple act (as Locard's Exchange Principle instructs) transfers DNA particles from one person to another. Small, even microscopic amounts of physical and/or biological material found at a crime scene is called *trace evidence.*

Trace evidence can come in the form of:

- Hair
- Skin cells
- Clothing
- Fibers
- Pollen
- Glass fragments or other forms of debris
- Pet hair or dander on rugs and/or carpets
- Paint chips
- Used facial tissue
- Blood stains on clothing (even as small as a tiny drop)
- Soil, dirt, or debris tracked into a house on shoes
- Hair on a hairbrush
- A toothbrush

Trace evidence that isn't readily visible to the eye must be gathered and examined under a powerful microscope.

Physical evidence includes things such as: tool marks, pry marks or gouges to a door or window sill, fibers, weapons, bullets, shell casings, fingerprints, and impressions of a vehicle tire or shoe.

One of the evidence-gathering "tricks of the trade" comes when a detective is interviewing a witness, a suspect, or person of interest. Before the interview, the detective will offer a drink or a cigarette to the person being questioned. While this gesture may seem like an attempt to be polite and try to build rapport with the person being questioned, it also can be a way to collect samples of DNA for laboratory analysis. These samples can be used to run a fingerprint search through the Automated Fingerprint Identity System (AFIS) and/or the National Crime Information Center (NCIC) to try to find a match for identification purposes of the perpetrator and/or victim.

As evidence collection goes, fingerprints have historically been one of the best forms of identification available. No two individuals have the same identifiable fingerprints. From medical science, it's known that identical twins possess the same DNA – or genetic codes – but they do not share the same fingerprints.

Fingerprints

The basic fingerprint patterns are *loop*, *whorl*, and *arch*. These three categories, each have subcategories:

- Loop
  - Ulnar Loop
  - Radial Loop
- Whorl
  - Plain Whorl
  - Central Pocket (Loop) Whorl
  - Double Loop Whorl
  - Accidental
- Arch
  - Plain Arch
  - Tented Arch

A whorl pattern has two *deltas*. In biometrics and latent print forensics, a delta is a pattern of a fingerprint that resembles a triangle, which is equivalent to the shape of the fourth letter of the Greek alphabet, the letter delta. It signifies change, or a change in the pattern of the ridge symmetry, design, and appearance of the fingerprint

Here are some examples:

Ulnar Loop

Radial Loop

Central Pocket (Loop) Whorl

Double Loop Whorl

Tented Arch

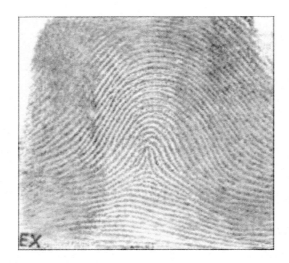

The 7 S's of Crime Scene Investigation

The basic steps of effective crime scene evidence collection can be referred to as the *7 S's of Crime Scene Investigation*.

Securing the Scene

The most important responsibility of the first officer at a crime scene is to attend to the safety of all individuals in the immediate area. Followed closely behind this task is to preserve evidence. However, securing the scene is the first of the 7 S's of Crime Scene Investigation, which represents the evidence collection process. The first officer on the scene must begin roping it off with crime scene tape or a similar barrier to prevent contamination of the scene by all unauthorized personnel. Great care must be taken to prevent any transferring or trampling at the scene, which could possibly contaminate or destroy crucial evidence. There are no second chances to collect evidence. Once the crime scene is torn down and turned over to the public, there are no "do overs."

Separating the Witnesses

So potential witnesses don't talk and compare their stories, *separating the witnesses* is the second of the 7 S's. Witnesses naturally want to talk and to hear what others may have seen or heard to attempt to bolster or disprove their own perceptions. Eyewitness testimony can be some of the least-reliable testimony because it is subject to considerable subjective interpretation. Separating the witnesses is crucial so that events that occurred will not be compared among them. Separating witnesses so that collusion (where witnesses work together to intentionally color the facts) doesn't occur is vital to preserve any evidence that witnesses may have to offer.

All of these activities flow naturally as the crime scene investigator must then continue to advance the process of evidence collection, since time is a crucial factor in the preservation of evidence. Different team members must play their roles simultaneously. For example, arriving detectives have to begin asking such questions as: Who called in the crime? Can anyone identify the perpetrator? Who saw something important? The detectives also have the task of going through the victim's personal items (his/her pockets and/or wallet or purse to attempt to identify the victim).

The medical examiner's investigators will want to try to establish what time the victim's death occurred.

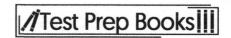

Scanning the Scene

Scanning the scene is the third of the Seven S's of Crime Scene Investigation.

The crime scene investigator must scan the scene to determine and decide where photos must be taken to preserve evidence — as it is where it lays — ultimately for later use at trial.

There may be a *primary crime scene* (defined as the location where the crime occurred; also referred to as a "hot scene") and a *secondary crime scene*, a location other than the primary scene but still very much related to the crime. This is where evidence also may be found and collected.

For example, a murder may have taken place at one location (the primary crime scene), but the body of the victim was found elsewhere (the secondary crime scene). Both scenes must be given the utmost care and attention, since each will bear fruitful evidence if the requisite time and attention are given to find, collect, extract, and preserve the evidence that has been left.

Seeing the Scene

Closely related to "scanning the scene" is the fourth of the 7 S's of Crime Scene Investigation and evidence collection, which is *seeing the scene.*

The investigator must "take in the big picture," meaning to "breathe it in" and visualize it simultaneously.

The investigator does this by taking photos of the entire crime scene — getting a "helicopter view" of all of the relevant evidence. These photos first must be taken with and then without the use of a ruler. Why is the use of a ruler part of this process?

This is done to establish the "triangulation," which is a means of establishing a distance or location by measuring the space between two fixed points whose exact location is known and a third unknown point, using the measurement of the angles between each point. The photos are taken establishing the triangulation between objects to establish clear reference points between fixed or stationary objects.

It is crucial that this is done from multiple vantage points or angles and from varying distances such as "close up" and wide shots so that perspective can be captured, and a 360-degree overview will be recorded for trial.

Sketching the Scene

The fifth S in the 7 S's in Crime Scene Investigation is *sketching the scene.*

Before beginning any sketch, it is imperative the sketch preparer, who completes sketches and is an essential member of the CSI team, obtains a comprehensive view of the scene. The preparer must establish the sketch limits and decide what to include and what to exclude. If the scene is overly complicated, a number of sketches may be necessary for adequate documentation.

The sketch preparer must:

- Diagram the immediate area of the crime scene.

- Identify and denote major items of evidence to sketch.

- Establish and mark clearly those areas to be searched and advise the team leader and all other search members of the items to be sketched so that no one interferes with the scene until the investigator's work is complete.

- Seek confirmation from a neutral second party for assistance for taking measurements and check twice that those measurements are accurate.

It is important to sketch all visual evidence. If the crime took place inside a structure, it's crucial to denote doors, doorways, hallways, window location, and any furniture that may be in the room. If the crime scene is outside, it's important to record the location of landmarks such as houses, buildings, and vehicles, and a special mention about any notable trees or other natural barriers.

The preparer must "paint the picture" and sketch what exists to scale. As well as photos and a written report, part of the essential ingredients of a thorough and effective crime scene reconstruction is sketches of the scene.

For example, an accurate initial rough draft at a murder scene is sketched denoting:

- The dead body — exactly where it fell and how it was configured when it hit the ground

- All other evidence

Each object should be measured from two fixed, immovable landmarks. Every sketch should begin by denoting north as indicated on the diagramed example previously shown. From that, all other directions are established (south, east, and west).

There are six basic types of sketches:

- Locality sketch: This is an overall "helicopter view" of the crime scene (not literally done from a helicopter). This is created to capture a wide-angle, broad-view perspective. It typically includes nearby buildings, connecting streets and/or surface roads leading into and out of the crime scene, and the exact location of the deceased in relationship to landmarks. This map will be more easily recognizable if one thinks of it as a "you are here" type of sketch.

- Grounds sketch: A grounds sketch is made when the intention is to show the crime scene in conjunction with the general area or surroundings. This sketch should show where the victim landed after being killed or after the crime took place and, like the previous sketch, all identifiable landmarks around him/her, such as buildings and/or businesses. If the criminal act was committed outside, the sketch should show the street on which the victim was found.

- Building sketch: This sketch differs in one regard from the grounds sketch: it is a sketch of the interior of a structure. If the crime took place inside a building, then the entire room needs to be sketched, indicating the location of the crime scene in relation to the other rooms in the structure. This sketch must accurately depict all of the rooms so that a person who has never set foot into the structure will have a good idea of the way the rooms are configured. This is similar to an engineer's or architect's blueprint floor plan, which shows doors, windows, hallways, etc.

- Location sketch: This shows the total crime scene, excluding the surrounding area as in the locality sketch. It depicts the crime scene tape and any barricades used to cordon off the area.

This sketch is similar to the building sketch but is more concerned with the actual crime scene than its position in relation to the surrounding environment.

- Detailed sketch: This is a drawing that shows an up-close and personal view of the evidence observed. This sketch is "zooming in" on everything that is present to the eye and relevant to the crime scene. This "zooming in" on the details is done so that the crime scene investigator can recreate the complete crime scene for the jury. This drawing is done in such a way to show three dimensions. It is often referred to as a *cross projection sketch*. It provides the observer with a multidimensional view of the room and a view of the evidence that is found on the floor as well as the walls — for example, an entry hole from a bullet. The observer is viewing the room from the ceiling, which makes the sketch appear three-dimensional.

- Finished drawing or sketch: This drawing is the final "masterpiece" from the sketch artist. This is what will be presented in court and is a polished work of art. This is typically completed using computer-automated design (CAD) technology. Any or all of the field sketches can be used as a reference for this final rendition. Permission will be asked of the sitting judge to enter this exhibit into evidence. The scale measures should be indicated clearly on the sketch. For smaller renditions, as a general rule of use: ½ inch = 1 foot for detailed sketches, and ¼ inch = 1 foot for larger crime scene sketches. Before trial, a clean final sketch should be created. There are companies whose sole purpose is to design clear, concise diagrams of evidence such as medical illustrations, 3D scale models, video recreations, and animation to prepare for trial. These computer-generated replicas make the case easier to understand, while proving to be highly captivating for a jury

All of the sketching is part of the chain of custody (CoC), which will be discussed later.

As may be apparent by now, professionals who have studied in the disciplines of mathematics, physics, physiology, chemistry, earth sciences, biology, criminal justice, and criminology are typically those who work in this area of law enforcement. A strong STEM (science, technology, engineering, and mathematics) background is highly sought after by agencies looking to hire a person in this area of specialization.

Searching for Evidence

The sixth of the Seven S's of Crime Scene Investigation is *searching for evidence*.

As in all areas of life, one must plan ahead. Preparation is the key to success. Poor prior planning will produce poor results, which can ruin a case.

One must plan a search for evidence before conducting the activity. Just as a traveler might map out a long-distance road trip by using a global positioning system (GPS) unit, a well-trained and experienced crime scene investigator must permit his or her training to guide the search for evidence.

Veteran search and rescue pilots for the U.S. Coast Guard search the vast oceans attempting to find debris from airplanes that have crashed. In order to work efficiently and not be duplicative in their efforts, these pilots often use a "grid pattern" to help ensure an organized, systematic, coordinated, and thorough search for evidence. It's similar to one of the ways used to search for evidence at a crime scene.

There are four basic crime scene search patterns:

- Strip or line search: Several investigators stand in one line and walk in the same direction or create lanes with ropes and stakes and individually scan each lane. This method is often used when looking for a large object in a large area.

- Grid: This is conducted like a strip search but in all directions, making it the most thorough search technique.

- Quadrant grid (also known as the zone grid): Zones or quadrants are covered by search team members, with slight overlaps in each section to avoid missing areas.

- Spiral search: A center stake has a rope attached to ensure that proper distance is maintained between loops of the spiral to avoid duplicating or missing areas that have been or have not been searched. This method is often employed when looking for gun shell cases or objects thrown at distances that are suspected to be at specific intervals from one another.

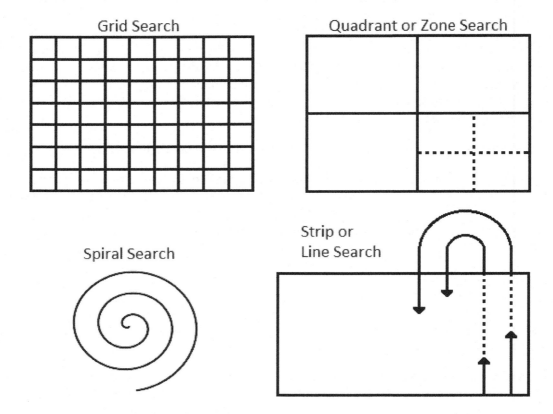

All of these pattern types are a network of lines that cross each other to form a series of squares or rectangles. These types are the most effective when they are walked, slowly, foot-by-foot, yard-by-yard, with as many sets of eyes and "boots on the ground" as the department can possibly employ. The pattern employed in a given situation depends on the specifics of the case.

Larger municipal police forces generally have more resources and trained personnel to apply to any crime scene investigation.

In smaller municipalities, where there are fewer resources and staff, one or a few officers may walk a simple grid, linear or spiral in nature. Conversely, larger departments with more resources and staff typically may initially use a *quadrant grid* search pattern. While all of these patterns are effective, the search will only be as effective as the personnel "walking the grid" with the utmost attention to detail.

These patterns are systematic and designed to leave no stone unturned.

The grid used to search should be walked at least by one other person, who brings an additional pair of eyes to the search and additional experience in a neutral and objective way. As each area is searched, it should be checked off so that time isn't wasted re-canvassing an area that has already been searched.

Securing and Collecting Evidence

Once an investigator has done adequate due diligence and conducted a full exhaustive search of the area, *securing and collecting evidence* is the seventh and final step in the Seven S's of Crime Scene Investigation. This comprises all the evidence that has been sketched, mapped, and uncovered.

The general approach to working a crime scene from arrival to tear down is as follows:

- Catch the call, prep a kit, and report to the scene
- Arrive on scene, report to dispatch, and tape off the scene
- Begin by conducting the 7 S's of crime scene and evidence collection and a step-by-step approach to conducting an on-scene search
- Approach the scene with care and caution
- Preserve, protect, and secure evidence
- Start preliminary canvassing of the crime scene
- Evaluate physical evidence
- Prep a brief narrative description
- Thoroughly photograph the scene
- Prepare sketches of the scene
- Conduct a detailed and systematic search
- Record and collect physical evidence
- Conduct a final survey
- Tear down the crime scene

The proper recording and collection of all evidence at a crime scene is the linchpin to a successful prosecution of any case.

It is essential that all evidence is packaged, secured, labeled, and stored with the utmost care and consideration.

The crime scene evidence recorder/custodian is the person responsible for bagging and tagging all evidence at a crime scene.

The evidence recorder/custodian must:

- Ensure the significant evidence is sketched and photographed before it's collected, since once it's collected, one can't backtrack and complete the task, so it should be done properly the first time.

- Describe evidence and its location on the appropriate bag or envelope containing it.

- Sign and date all evidence containers, maintaining the chain of custody.

- Appropriately collect and package evidence to maximize evidence integrity.

- Maintain a detailed evidentiary log.

- Always employ the use of appropriate protective equipment (latex gloves) and methods when dealing with potentially infectious biohazard evidence such as blood, semen, or fecal matter.

Rigorous protocols governing this task of this team member must be adhered to with meticulous detail, since the packaging of evidence is extremely crucial to its preservation.

If a piece of evidence is bagged improperly (e.g., not secured properly to keep out air or other contaminants), it is probable that the entire sample could be lost forever, rendering it useless.

In general, physical evidence must be submitted according to the following guidelines:

A. Basic Packaging
Here are some guidelines for packaging evidence:

- All evidence, including firearms, should be submitted in a tamper-evident, sealed container or package.

- Evidence storage bags must have self-sealing capabilities. The evidence gatherer's initials must appear on the seal(s).

- All other plastic bags used for packaging evidence (e.g., those not self-sealing) must be heat-sealed and initialed directly over the seal.

- Plastic bags not specifically manufactured for evidence storage will not be accepted if sealed with evidence tape, since this type of seal can be easily compromised.

All evidence gathered in a liquid state must be contained in a shatter-resistant container with a locking lid.

Two of the most common types of liquids found at crime scenes are blood and semen.

Biological evidence in its liquid form, such as blood and semen, are best preserved when stored in containers that permit the free flow of air to cause the samples to dry out, thus reducing the likelihood of the evidence sample will be degraded beyond use due to the fact that it was contaminated by mold growth.

Wet evidence should not be folded onto other areas of clothing. Best practices dictate that a shirt be placed on a coat hanger to prevent cross-contamination with other areas of the garment. This will insulate blood stain patterns from contamination and transfer.

All suspected bodily fluid stains found at the scene must be submitted to the lab for analysis. In order to prevent cross-contamination from taking place, do not allow any of the victim(s) clothing to come in contact with the person of interest (POI) or a subsequent suspect. One goal as a crime scene investigator and evidence gatherer is to collect the evidence in the state that it was found in. If the evidence was still

in its liquid state, then collect it wet. If it has dried, then it must be "scraped off" the surface it rests on in order to preserve it for subsequent analysis at the crime lab.

B. Methods of Collection in General

Best practices dictate that a long-stemmed cotton swab should be used in the gathering and recovering of any and all biological evidence, regardless of whether the evidence samples are in a liquid or dried state.

Similarly, much like how a chef would baste a turkey in the kitchen to prepare it for Thanksgiving, in the crime scene investigator's kit, there should be a "bulb and syringe" or a "baster" to collect any liquid of evidentiary value in conjunction with the cotton swab.

The evidence gatherer should always:

- Wear gloves on both hands to ensure protection from biological hazards and to properly protect and preserve the evidence.

- If collecting a dry specimen (for example, dried blood), gently moisten the long-stemmed cotton swabs with distilled water to allow saturation. If collecting a wet specimen, the tip will likely not need to be moistened with water.

- With a slight pressure and even stroking motion, thoroughly rub the stain using only one swab per stain when it is small in overall size and employing multiple cotton swabs for larger area surface evidentiary stains.

- Employ the tip of the cotton swab if there is only a microscopic trace that needs to be gathered.

- Permit all evidentiary cotton swabs to air dry naturally with time.

- Be certain to separately place each individual cotton swab or swatch in wholly and completely separate packages, and then place each package inside a paper envelope.

Paper bags similar to (but more durable) than brown lunch bags work the best in the packaging of evidence. Paper hinders degradation. The paper bag should then be placed inside another paper bag and sealed with tape. The initials of the evidence collector must be written across the tape.

Following these essentials, one must begin an evidence log, which is a vital "chain of custody" document that must be attached to the bagged evidence.

All of the following information should be indicated clearly on the evidence log:

- Case number

- A description of the evidence contained therein

- The specific and separate number that must be assigned in the inventory process for the specific item collected

- The date and time the evidence was collected.

- The name of the person of interest (POI) or suspect (if that information is available)

- A signature bearing the full name of the person who collected the evidence

- A signature bearing the full name of any witness or witnesses who were present when the evidence was collected

Tamper-evident collection should include the following guidelines:

- A heat seal must be on any "zip-lock" or other plain plastic bag not specifically designed for evidence collection.

- Paper bags and envelopes must be taped end to end, over the opening.

- Staples alone are not sufficient to provide tamper-evidence capability since they can be removed and then reinserted.

- Metal cans of evidence must be taped over the top and on opposing sides (e.g., over the lid and down both sides of the container), so that any cutting of the tape is evident by the fact that the tape is not in one continual piece.

- Specially manufactured evidence storage bags (Tyvek, plastic, etc.) must be sealed with material that cannot be opened without being destroyed to provide an indication about whether it has been opened.

- Tamper-evident tape should always be evidence tape that will not remain intact upon its removal.

Computers should have evidence tape placed over the power supply slot and over all disk, CD, DVD, and backup tape slots. Initials shall be placed on the tape and seal(s).

All outer packaging or containers must be labeled with:

- Submitting agency case number
- Name/initials/badge number of seizing officer
- Description of item
- Item number
- Date and time seized

Keep in mind that an evidentiary control or "control sample" and prints will need to be taken from the victim to establish potential exclusion. Blood samples that are gathered from the primary crime scene will need to be taken back to the laboratory and cross-typed and matched with the blood samples from the victim's body. If a positive match is established between the two sources, then those specific blood samples are excluded from further analysis. Likewise, if the blood samples turn out not to be a match, then they may have come from the perpetrator.

In order to present evidence in court that is admissible, the integrity of the evidence from the crime scene must be preserved throughout the collection process. This includes the transfer and storage processes, and the laboratory analysis of said evidence — all the way to the day the matter goes to trial.

Chain of Custody

This process is known as the *chain of custody (CoC)*. The chain of custody is a rigorous and detailed process that is crucial to a successful investigation.

The chain of custody can be thought of as similar to the baton passes in a track and field relay race. Each member of the relay team runs a portion of the race. At the conclusion of a specific portion, each runner (except the last) is responsible for handing the baton to the next runner, who will cover the next specific measured distance. The same applies for the crime scene investigatory team.

The chain of custody is often thought of as a concept, but it is also a written log — an evidentiary tracking document. Its inception takes place when an officer, detective, or investigator initially arrives at the scene of the crime. The chain's purpose is to establish a seamless history and step-by-step reconstruction of all actions taken at a crime scene, from initial observation, to the hand-written notes of observations of the evidence (at the crime scene), to the collection, processing, analysis, and delivery of evidence from the crime scene to the courtroom.

In order to effectively establish the chain of custody, direct evidence must be put on at trial that clearly and unequivocally shows that the evidence has remained intact, uncorrupted, and is trustworthy.

In the courtroom, witnesses of "the chain" will be called to testify on the (witness) stand and under oath while facing the penalty of perjury. Questions that are typically presented include the following:

- Who collected the evidence?
- What is the evidence (a description)?
- When was it collected?
- Where was it collected?
- How was it collected?

The manifest must match its content. The evidence being testified about must actually be in the bag. This process of validation and verification of the bagged evidentiary items must be established. This is crucial to the chain of custody process and a crucial part of the authentication and verification of evidence.

Chain of custody actions consist of the following:

- Detailed notetaking (which focuses on a description of the evidence observed and collected. These facts must include the condition in which the item(s) were found, the location, day, date, and time that the items of evidence were logged and any unusual markings or findings related to an item of evidence).

- Written statements as to the efforts to preserve and collect the evidence, as well as a written record of how the evidence was gathered, and how it was processed and packaged

- A written account of the process taken to seal and secure the evidence

- A written account of every piece of evidence gathered

- Preparation of the chain of custody documentation

The prosecution typically needs the assistance of members of the CSI team, who can:

- Testify that the evidence being proffered at trial is the exact same evidence that the crime scene investigator collected and/or received.

- State the specific day, date, and time that the evidence was received or transferred to another team member for further processing in the chain of custody.

- Certify that there absolutely was no tampering with the item while it was in custody.

The chain of custody process lays the foundation for the admission of evidence. After laying the foundation, the attorney will:

- Request permission from the judge to have the court reporter mark each exhibit (piece of evidence) for identification.

- Proffer or put on testimony identifying or describing each exhibit.

- Offer into evidence the exhibit as part of the official record of the proceedings.

- Allow the opposing counsel to examine the evidence, giving them a chance to object.

- Submit each exhibit to the court for the judge to possibly examine.

- Allow for a ruling on the admissibility rendered from the bench on each piece of evidence.

- Request permission to present each exhibit and, if admitted, to the jury by reading a description to them and showing it to them.

Why go through such a labor-intensive process, one might ask?

The Fourth Amendment to the U.S. Constitution prohibits the government from unreasonable searches and seizures or the illegal gathering of evidence. These thoroughly scrutinized details are essential in order to authenticate and subsequently introduce evidence in a court of law.

The collection of evidence is governed by a rigorous set of formal standards and stringent protocols established by the courts and codified into law to protect and preserve the integrity of evidence samples. This helps ensure they can be fairly and impartially used in a court of law to adjudicate guilt or innocence. There are rules that govern both civil trials and criminal trials for the use and introduction of evidence in the courtrooms across the United States.

Trial Exhibits

A crucial aspect to evidence collection is being able to use that evidence in a court of law. Cases are often won and lost by the successful challenges to the evidence that is presented at trial.

No evidence is admissible unless it first has been *authenticated*. The authentication process is the linchpin to being permitted to show the evidence to the jury. Without evidence being authenticated through the chain of custody process, the evidence collected is worthless.

Here are some key points about introducing and authenticating exhibits at the trial level:

- The general requirement of authentication or identification is satisfied by the person offering the evidence that it is what it is claimed to be. He or she must be able to testify under oath to such things as:

  o "I am the person who picked up the murder weapon."

  o "I placed the gun into this plastic bag."

  o "I sealed the bag."

  o "Those are my initials on the tape that is on the bag."

- The burdens of production and persuasion are on the person offering the evidence.

- The judge shall decide if the evidence will be admitted or not.

- The jury ultimately decides on the authenticity of the evidence.

The chain of custody can be broken when an evidence custodian of the crime scene investigation team neglects to do simple things such as:

- Sign his or her name or initials on the evidence bag.

- Indicate the day, date, and time that the evidence was collected.

- Provide the specific case number that was assigned to the case on every piece of evidence collected.

Carelessness such as this helps open the door to successful challenges to the admissibility of the evidence collected. As mentioned, success at the trial level comes from effectively being able to challenge the admissibility of evidence that the prosecution wishes to introduce.

A single effective challenge to a single crucial piece of evidence (for example, the murder weapon in a homicide case) can be sufficient to create enough doubt in the jury's mind to bring about an acquittal.

Sloppy evidence collection techniques, practices, and protocols assist the defense at trial. Cases that may appear to be "air-tight" legally have imploded due to a single and solitary broken link in the chain of custody. It is a high price to pay, especially if and when the legal concept of "double jeopardy" applies, and the accused cannot by law be tried twice for the same crime.

If the evidence can't be explained clearly and convincingly to the jury, if the chain of custody has inexplicable breaks in it, or if it has holes in it like a piece of Swiss cheese, this will provide ample room for even a rookie defense attorney to establish doubt as to the integrity of the evidence being presented against his or her client.

With today's advanced technology, bar codes are used to track every piece of evidence collected. Crime scene team leaders onsite are required to control the scene, leaving nothing to chance or the good intentions of other crucial players in the investigatory process. A seasoned crime scene investigator should question his or her own work, employing a discerning and critical eye to every action undertaken at the scene. The investigator should anticipate potential legal challenges that typically arise and work from an internal viewpoint that "if this evidence is going to be admitted, it is up to me to collect and preserve it properly."

In many jurisdictions, recently hired or trainee team members (those who have less than a year on the job) are typically required to observe and learn.

A great deal can be learned from errors in collecting evidence. Such errors teach crime scene investigators what not to do.

One famous example of the sort of problems that may arise at trial when the chain of custody is broken or even open to questions is *The People v. Orenthal James (O.J.) Simpson*. Multiple successful challenges by Simpson's legal defense team to the evidence were sufficient enough for the jury to come back with a not guilty verdict.

Today, this case is used as a benchmark for analysis and further study to attempt to help further the field of forensics and how to properly go about conducting the crucial job of evidence collection.

Working backward, before any evidence has its "day in court," it must first have been collected, preserved, sketched, photographed, and transported to a secure storage locker, where it will most likely sit for a significant period of time before there is any hint or hope of a trial. The concept of a "speedy trial" is, unfortunately, more of a theory than a practice. As we have stressed before, considerable time can pass, even years potentially, from the time of the crime to the courtroom.

Television has spoiled many people into thinking that a murder can be solved in one hour. This is hardly the case. Murders cannot be solved in an hour. Television has also colored the facts of the general public about whether there should be or will be clear and unequivocal DNA results in every court case. This, as well, simply is not reality.

Tests on the evidence are made, analyses are undertaken, and sometimes, unfortunately, a DNA match is not found.

Evidence Storage

Prior to submitting evidence to an accredited criminal analysis laboratory for rigorous testing, evidence is transferred to an evidence room for storage. It's essential that a secure transfer of evidence occurs.

It's also of the utmost importance that the following associated evidence information is recorded accurately and in detail:

- The case number issued by the police department with jurisdiction over where the crime was committed

- The address where the incident occurred

- A clear description of the evidence

- The name, rank, and badge number of the officer who observed the evidence at the scene

- The name of the lead detective(s) responsible for investigating the case

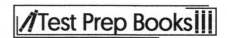

- The signature of the officer who delivered the specific evidence, with the date affixed to the evidence log-in sheet

- The name, rank, and badge number of the officer who transported the evidence to the evidence locker and into the care, control, and custody of the evidence custodian

As an example, the list of evidence can include the following:

- Sequential number of each evidentiary item
- Quantity of items included (e.g., 20 spent shell casings)
- Serial number of the item in question (e.g., a handgun)
- Description of item
- Status of the item, such as:
    o Ready to submit for analysis
    o Hold
    o Releasable (also referred to as RTC or return to claimant)

As an essential component of the investigatory and chain of evidence process, every municipality must work diligently to establish an *evidence management system (EMS)*. The municipality should be dedicated to ensuring the unyielding implementation of stringent protocols and strict controls regarding all evidence. All efforts need to be focused on the proper and lawful handling, securing, and disposal of evidence and/or property so that the citizenry whom the Office of Prosecutor or District Attorney serves will always have trust, faith, and confidence in the work undertaken in their name.

The person who is charged with such duties typically carries the official title of property or evidence custodian and has the following duties and responsibilities:

- Receives into custody (date and time stamping) evidence, which can include any property such as paperwork regarding seized vehicles, weapons (physically delivered to the property room), seized drugs and paraphernalia, as well as recovered and/or abandoned property, etc.

- Disposes of evidence and property when it has served its purpose after a legal matter has been adjudicated at the trial level

- Provides expert testimony in a court of law to certify the chain of evidence when ordered to do so by a judge

- Responds occasionally to crime scenes to gather and secure evidence into custody

In general, an evidence custodian must meet certain minimum qualifications. In most municipalities, for example, a candidate must possess these minimum qualifications:

- High school diploma or GED equivalent

- Three years of experience in a law enforcement agency in the collection, preservation, safeguarding, and disposal of evidence and property, or two years of full-time experience as a sworn law enforcement officer

- Hold a valid vehicle operator's license

The responsibilities of property or evidence custodians are crucial in the evidence collection process. If someone had the opportunity to tag-along or was able to follow an evidence custodian through a typical "day in the cage" (at work), one would observe him or her being responsible for the following:

- Directly liaising with law enforcement officers

- Receiving or taking into custody abandoned and/or found property

- Properly "logging in" evidence from any officer for potential use afterward at the trial level or for subsequent further analysis. A custodian may be required to maintain some form of computer information management system (CIMS), as well as a handwritten double-entry paper recording system to ensure accuracy and clarity of what the evidence room actually has in it. The CIMS is an electronic database registry used to conduct information-gathering background searches of any and all relevant or related parties (next of kin, etc.) and investigate and identify who may be the rightful owner of certain property items in the agency's possession. This enables the return of this property to the rightful owner in accordance with proclaimed rules and regulations of any governing statutes or court procedures for the locality of the agency.

- Providing evidence when ordered by a judge to do so for proceedings in a courtroom (e.g., certifying the chain of custody regarding the evidence)

- Diligently maintaining all appropriate records

When ordered to do so, the custodian also must perform these actions:

- Dispose or release evidence upon issuance of court rulings

- Conduct thorough and random audits and inventories of evidence to verify the available internal records and to establish their correctness, accuracy, and location within the system

- Maintain requisite detailed records on evidence and found property

- Input data in a computer database

- Prepare detailed written reports

- Receive seized vehicles into custody

- Maintain and operate a vehicle impound lot

The evidence custodian should be well-versed in legal issues regarding the rules of procedure in submitting evidence in a court proceeding. This person must be:

- Flexible in his or her work schedule, since it may be required to occasionally work a variety of hours that are randomly subject to change with very little to no prior notice.

- Able to work without supervision.

- Capable of lifting heavy boxes that may be filled with evidence.

At an agency-wide operational level, the evidence custodian will need to be able to organize, plan, and coordinate the work environment, being effective with verbal communication and possessing professional writing skills.

There are three types of cases that the property room/evidence room maintains:

- Active case files: cases that have yet to be determined by a judge or jury

- Closed case files: cases that have been adjudicated

- Cold case files: cases representing criminal acts that have no resolution in a court of law. In these cases, sufficient time has passed without the case being cracked or solved, thus all leads have gone "cold." Here are some situations that can bring a cold case back into activity: new information; a credible lead, such as a witness who previously wasn't available stepping forward; newly discovered DNA evidence; or a perceived return to criminality by a person of interest or suspect as evidenced by more victims.

These files are generally kept by the evidence custodian in a binder and organized and controlled by the year and the specific property number for the case.

An accurate computer database should be maintained indicating the following:

- Location of each item of evidence in the evidence warehouse
- Current status of all relevant case evidence

Ninety days after the official disposition, all property shall be returned to its rightful owner or properly disposed. All documents relevant to the case should be forwarded to the Office of the District Attorney to be included in the original case file. Those documents that are not included in the original case file and turned over to the Prosecutor's Office shall be returned to the investigating officer so that they can be included in his or her case notes for reference.

Forensic Science

The successful investigation and prosecution of criminal acts generally requires the collection, recording, preservation, and forensic analysis of evidence. This critical analysis is the indisputable key to reaching a determination of guilt or innocence.

The field of forensic science has come a long way in a relatively short period of time. The last 20 years has brought the mission of solving crime and the field of forensic science to new and enhanced levels, giving forensic science a host of the most modern tools to continue the never-ending quest to solve crime and bring about justice for all parties.

The mission of every crime laboratory should be to provide the highest-quality, most-timely, accurate, and reliable forensic services and results by using state-of-the-art best practices, protocols, and controls in conjunction with the best technology available. A good crime laboratory must focus on delivering unbiased results and always being transparent in the pursuit of furthering the cause of justice.

Forensics is the application of science and technology to the field of law. Forensic science is comparative in nature and focuses on comparing one control sample with another for the purpose of investigating and prosecuting criminal acts through the use of science and technology.

The goal of any director of a forensic laboratory should be to operate the lab in such a way that it earns the accreditation of the American Society of Crime Laboratory Directors Laboratory Accreditation Board. This accreditation is one of the most prestigious that a laboratory can earn.

Many people may be old enough to remember seeing the world-renowned Dr. Henry C. Lee testifying under oath on the witness stand in *The People v. Orenthal James (O.J.) Simpson* in the mid-1990s. At the time, Dr. Lee served as the chief criminalist for the state of Connecticut, as well as the esteemed director of the Police Forensic Laboratory for the State Police in Connecticut. In this specific trial, he appeared as a paid independent consultant, not in any official capacity with either of the entities referenced above.

Dr. Lee has made enormous contributions in furthering the field of forensics through the tireless pioneering work that he has dedicated himself to throughout his long and stellar career. He was even asked to re-examine the forensics surrounding the assassination of John Fitzgerald Kennedy, the 35th president of the United States.

While Dr. Lee is an example of the highest achievement in the field, the vast majority of forensic laboratory work is done every day by far lower profile (but equally important) professionals who hold titles such as chemist, criminalist, scientist, lab tech, serologist, toxicologist, or specialist (to name just a few). These professionals have dedicated themselves to the pursuit of justice.

Although they routinely work away from the spotlight of high-profile, televised trials, the discharge of their daily duties is crucial in the evidence collection process. These duties include, but are not limited to, the following technical services:

- Examine and evaluate all physical evidence collected by law enforcement agencies at the scene of a crime or that may be related to a crime

- Ensure the safety of those who are charged with the examination of the evidence, while at the same time protecting and preserving the integrity and safe handling of the evidence in the lab's custody

- Be able to submit written reports of the results of examinations to the law enforcement agency that requested the testing

- Seek and employ the qualified services of other experts when necessary and when third-party, independent expert opinions are requested

- Provide personnel from within internal ranks who can offer expert forensic testimony as to any evidence at issue

- Cooperate and collaborate in crime scene re-construction and processing when requested to do so

- Actively manage a curriculum of training courses in forensic criminal investigation on an annual basis for all area-wide law enforcement agencies (for example, conducting police training academy classes for incoming recruits)

- Do everything possible to advance the specialty of forensics by conducting regular and continual research in forensic sciences

All of this work must be performed within the Quality Assurance Standards for Forensic DNA Processing Labs, which has been established by the Federal Bureau of Investigation (FBI), and the stringent protocols in accordance with the International Standards Organization (ISO) standard 17025. It should be noted that the Federal Bureau of Investigation (FBI) operates one of the largest and most comprehensive forensic laboratories in the world.

Some of the "next generation" and more advanced technologies that have revolutionized the field of forensic science can be employed in the lab to help establish guilt or innocence. Here are some examples of this high-tech equipment.

Probability Analysis Software

This innovative software has given birth to the concept of "predictive policing." It is employed to mine tremendous amounts of quantitative information. This "data mining" is then used to analyze, interpret, and maximize manpower efficiency and output and to forecast predictions about where crime is likely to occur and where suspects are likely to be located, thus helping to prevent crime. It can also be used to aid in solving open cases.

Integrated Automated Fingerprint Identification System (IAFIS)

As crime and the criminals who do such deeds sometimes seldom sleep, the IAFIS system never takes a break – it's always operating. Employed globally, the system is in operation around the clock every day of the year to help international, federal, state, and local law enforcement agencies to verify and validate evidence that has been submitted, to aide in properly identifying persons of interest (POI) or suspects, and bring them to justice in a court of law.

The IAFIS system is the most comprehensive evidence-gathering electronic criminal fingerprint database in the world. The computer does all of the work. With a single click of the "enter" button, it can automatically access more than 70 million historical criminal records and histories, as well as a photo or "mugshot" of a suspect on file.

Carbon 14 Forensic Dating

This application is used to determine the age of an object by measuring the trace element carbon, which exists in all living things.

3D Facial Reconstruction (FR) Database Software

This is also known as 3D Biometric Facial Marker Recognition. It's highly useful in multiple applications, such as personal identification, access control of employees to high-security areas, and finding missing and kidnapped persons. For example, when a young child goes missing, 3D Facial Reconstruction (FR) Database Software is an important evidence-gathering tool that can be employed to capture the last known visible likeness of the child. Through the use of extensive mapping and morphing technology, the software can produce an age progression likeness of the child, showing what the child should resemble after aging. This helps law enforcement to develop a missing child bulletin to ask for help from the public and locate the person in the photo.

DNA Sequencer

More powerful than the related DNA profiling technique, this piece of sophisticated equipment is used to determine the order of the four foundational chemical building blocks referred to as "bases." Even with samples that have been degraded, DNA sequencing enables scientists to analyze human remains to determine the chemical structure of a DNA molecule. By knowing this chemical structure, scientists can then identify a suspect or victim with very minimal – even microscopic amounts – of trace evidence.

Video Spectral Comparator

This piece of advanced technology is an imaging device that permits a laboratory technician to analyze ink (such as the ink on currency) in order to make visible common hidden security features to the human eye and potentially reveal evidence that a document or bill has been altered. This technology is used extensively in the effort to combat the worldwide problem of counterfeit currency on the black market.

High-Speed Ballistics Photography

Another essential tool in the toolbox of the crime laboratory is a high-speed camera that can provide clear and unequivocal evidence used to slow the path of a bullet fired from a handgun. This provides the bullet's exact trajectory or pathway as it entered the victim's body. It can also show the shatter pattern of glass when it is broken in order to provide the directional manner of impact, which is especially effective in automobile crime scene reconstruction.

Alternative Light Photography

When used in conjunction with chemicals such as luminol, and when observed under an alternative to white light, such as those listed below, alternative light photography can enable an investigator to visualize things (e.g., blood, urine, semen, saliva, bruising under the skin, etc.) that are invisible to the naked eye and that the perpetrator hoped would remain unseen.

Some examples of alternative light are:

- Ultraviolet (UV black light)
- Blue light
- Argon-ion lasers
- Light-emitting diodes (LEDs)

Laser Ablation Inductively Coupled Plasma Mass Spectrometry (LA-ICP-MS)

In its simplest terms, LA-ICP-MS is an extremely powerful analytical tool that enables a laser beam to perform delicate elemental and isotopic analysis on solid samples of evidence. A unique aspect of this technology is that it can perform chemical analysis down to parts per billion – a capability that surpasses all previous microscopic crime fighting analysis.

Atomic Absorption Spectroscopy (AAS)

AAS is a potent tool for analyzing over 70 trace elements in a given sample through the use of absorbed radiation.

Retinal Scanner

Retinal scanners focus on the retina, which is the mirror-like surface on the back surface of the eye that processes light entering through the pupil. This technology analyzes the intricate and unique pattern of spindles of the blood vessels in the retina. The foundational principle of this technology is that these vessels provide a rare and unique pattern, which can be used as a tamper-resistant personal identifying marker.

Cyanoacrylate Fuming Chamber

Cyanoacrylate fuming chambers are employed in the crime laboratory to safely develop latent fingerprints.

This technology uses superheated vapors of a substance similar to "super glue." This substance adheres to the ridge patterns of latent fingerprints on various kinds of evidence, making fingerprints that would otherwise remain invisible visible to the eye.

Practice Questions

1. A crime has occurred. When exactly does the evidence collection process begin?
    a. When the police arrive on the scene
    b. When the crime scene investigators arrive on the scene
    c. When the chief of detectives arrives on the scene
    d. When the 911 dispatch officer takes the initial phone call regarding the crime, even before the police and EMS arrive on the scene

2. The foundational principle of Criminal Forensics studies to this day was established by Dr. Edmond Locard of Lyon, France. Locard's Exchange Principle basically states that:
    a. When a person comes in contact with another person, there is typically no transfer of physical evidence.
    b. When a person comes in contact with another person and one person has a head cold – the other party will be infected with his/her cold virus germs.
    c. When a person comes in contact with another person, place, or thing, a transfer of physical evidence can occur.
    d. When a person transfers evidence to the next person in the chain of custody, certain procedures must be followed.

3. What is evidence?
    a. The substance of things hoped for
    b. The available body of facts or information indicating or tending to prove whether a belief or theory is true or valid
    c. Only the things that you can observe with your own eyes
    d. All of the above

4. 3D Facial Reconstruction (FR) Database Software, also known as 3D Biometric Facial Marker Recognition, is highly useful in applications such as:
    a. Personal identification
    b. Access control of employees in high-security areas
    c. Finding missing and kidnapped persons
    d. All of the above

5. When gathering evidence, investigators should always use the proper equipment in order to accomplish their onsite tasks of evidence collection. Some of the items that are considered standard and are housed within the investigator's "kit" are listed below.
    Which item is NOT considered standard?
    a. Cotton swabs
    b. A large bucket with a locking lid
    c. Thermometer
    d. Healthy snacks

6. What are the four basic categories of evidence in forensics?
    a. Indirect, cyclical, trace, and transferrable
    b. Illogical, cynical, tracking, and photographic
    c. Direct, circumstantial, trace, and physical
    d. Diffused, clinical, testimonial, and eyewitness

7. How many different patterns of loop fingerprint patterns are there and what are they called?
    a. Four (plain, central, double, accidental)
    b. Two (ulnar, radial)
    c. One (arch)
    d. Three (whole, tented, spotted)

8. The CSI team leader (usually a high-ranking law enforcement officer) is responsible for the thorough, precise, and efficient legal collection and processing of all evidence left at the crime scene and elsewhere to solve a crime. Which of the following responsibilities listed below are NOT customarily part of the CSI team leader's tasks?
    a. Leading the preliminary walk-through of the crime scene
    b. Disposes of evidence and property when it has served its purpose after a legal matter has been adjudicated at the trial level
    c. Ensuring that all protocols are followed and strictly adhered to with no exceptions, such as protecting his or her team from blood products or other bio-hazard material that may be harmful to the health of those assigned to the crime scene
    d. Dictating assignments to the team of investigators

9. What is the chain of custody (CoC)?
    a. It is often thought of as a concept, but it is also a written log – an evidentiary tracking document.
    b. It is a double-reinforced series of chains that prevent any prisoner from escaping while in the custody of law enforcement officials.
    c. It is a way that convicted felons, who are sentenced to conduct community service, are chained together when they are going from the prison to the vehicles that will take them to their worksite.
    d. None of the above.

10. The property room (also referred to as the evidence room) generally maintains which three types of case files?
    a. Active case files, closed case files, and cold case files
    b. Active case files, closed case files, and warm case files
    c. Active case files, dead case files, and closed case files
    d. All of the above

11. Dr. Henry Lee is just one example of a well-seasoned and highly experienced professional who has made enormous contributions in furthering his field and area of specialization. Name the area of specialization that he has labored to advance and two of the major cases he has contributed to throughout his long and stellar career.
    a. Forensics and The People v. Orenthal J. (O.J.) Simpson and the Assassination of President John F. Kennedy
    b. Physics and Plessey v. Ferguson and the Assassination of President Abraham Lincoln
    c. Chemistry and Mapp v. Ohio and the Assassination of President James A. Garfield
    d. Rocket science and Brown v. The Board of Education and the Assassination of Robert Kennedy

12. Which list below shows the four basic pattern types used to search crime scenes?
    a. Grid, strip, linear, spiral
    b. Strip, circular, wavy, spiral
    c. Grid, strip, quadrant, spiral
    d. Wavy, strip, quadrant, spiral

13. Which is NOT one of the six kinds of sketches used in crime scene investigation and reconstruction?
    a. Locality
    b. Detailed
    c. Finished
    d. Scientific

14. What does the acronym IAFIS stand for?
    a. Integral Automated Fingerprint Identification System
    b. Identifiable Automated Fingerprint Integrity System
    c. Integrated Automated Fingerprint Identification System
    d. None of the above

15. The Video Spectral Comparator is used in the lab to do which of the following?
    a. Determine the order of the four foundational chemical building blocks more commonly referred to as "bases."
    b. Enable a laser beam to perform delicate elemental and isotopic analysis on solid samples of evidence.
    c. Provide clear and unequivocal evidence that can be used to slow the path of a bullet fired from a handgun, thus showing the bullet's exact trajectory or pathway as it entered the victim's body.
    d. Permit a laboratory technician to analyze ink, such as the ink on currency.

Answer Explanations

1. D: After a crime, the clock has started on a crucial chain of events, so every second counts. The first 48 hours are considered the "golden hours" in investigating and collecting evidence in any criminal case. The 911 dispatch officer's initial goal is to collect as much detailed informational evidence (oral evidence) from the caller to answer some very basic but important questions. What is your emergency? Where is your emergency located?

2. C: When a person comes in contact with a person, place, or thing, a transfer of physical evidence typically occurs. For example, when someone kisses, shakes hands, or sneezes (producing an ionized particle spray field), physical evidence is easily spread. This is all part of Locard's Exchange Principle about the transfer of physical evidence. This theory is the foundational principle upon which criminal forensics is built.

3. B: Evidence is the available body of facts or information indicating or tending to prove whether a belief or theory is true or valid. Evidence is corroborated, and substantiated proof that is entered under strict rules of admission in a court of law goes helps determine the outcome of a matter being contested.

4. D: When a young child goes missing, 3D Facial Reconstruction (FR) Database Software is an important evidence gathering tool that can be employed to capture the last known visible likeness of that child. Through the use of extensive mapping and morphing technology, an image can be produced that shows an age-progression likeness of the child. This helps law enforcement to develop a missing child bulletin and possibly receive help from the public to locate the child. It also can be used for access control security purposes and personal identification.

5. D: A crime scene investigator's kit includes items that are frequently used at the scene of the crime to help with the investigation. Common items include cotton swabs, latex or nitrate gloves, tweezers, paper or plastic bags, a surgical scalpel, a thermometer, and a large bucked with a locking lid to store liquids. While an investigator may keep healthy snacks on hand in his or her vehicle, food is not included in the investigative kit, especially because it might become contaminated with dangerous specimens.

6. C: Direct evidence is first-hand knowledge, first-person observations, eyewitness accounts, or video footage from police body or dashboard cameras. Circumstantial evidence is indirect evidence that can be used to infer a fact. Trace evidence is small, even microscopic amounts of physical and/or biological material. Physical evidence includes such things as tool marks, pry marks or gouges to a door or window sill, fibers, weapons, bullets, and shell casings, as well as impressions of a vehicle or shoe, and fingerprints.

7. B: There are two types of loop fingerprint patterns: ulnar, which relates to a turning toward the ulna bone in the forearm on the side opposite the thumb, and radial, which turns outward toward the radius bone of the arm on the thumb side.

8. B: Disposing of evidence and property when it has served its purpose after a legal matter has been adjudicated at the trial level is the job of the property or evidence custodian not generally the CSI team leader.

9. A: The chain of custody (CoC) is often thought of as a concept, but it is also a written log — an evidentiary tracking document. Its inception takes place when an officer, detective, or investigator initially arrives at the scene of the crime. Its purpose is to establish a seamless history and step-by-step reconstruction of all actions taken at a crime scene, from initial observation, to the hand-written notes of observations of the evidence (at the crime scene), to the collection, processing, analysis, and delivery of evidence from the crime scene to the courtroom. In order to effectively establish the chain of custody, direct evidence must be put on at trial that clearly and unequivocally shows that the evidence has remained intact, uncorrupted, and is trustworthy.

10. A: Regarding the types of cases that the property room/evidence room maintains, there are three types of cases: active, closed, and cold. These files are generally kept by the evidence custodian in a binder and organized and controlled by the year and the specific property number for the case. Active case files are those cases that have yet to be determined by a judge or jury. Closed case files are those that have been adjudicated. Cold case files are those involving criminal acts that have no resolution in a court of law.

11. A: Dr. Henry C. Lee has made enormous contributions in furthering the field of forensics through his tireless pioneering work. He also was asked to testify under oath on the witness stand in *The People v. Orenthal J. (O.J.) Simpson* and was asked to re-examine the forensics surrounding the assassination of John Fitzgerald Kennedy, the 35th president of the United States.

12. C: There are four basic search patterns that help with systematic investigation so that searches remain efficient yet thorough. The specific pattern employed depends on the specifics of the situation. Strip or line searches are used when investigators are looking for a large object in a large area. Grid patterns are even more thorough, so the item may be smaller or less conspicuous. Quadrant and spiral searches may also be instituted to ensure all area is covered.

13. D: A scientific sketch is NOT among the six sketches completed regarding a crime scene. A locality sketch is an overall "helicopter view." A grounds sketch shows the crime scene in conjunction with the general area or surroundings. A building sketch shows the interior of a structure. A location sketch shows the total crime scene, excluding the surrounding area as in the locality sketch. A detailed sketch shows a very up-close and personal view of the evidence observed. Lastly, the finished drawing or sketch is the final polished "masterpiece" from the sketch artists and is what will be presented in court. This is typically completed by using computer-automated design (CAD) technology.

14. C: Integrated Automated Fingerprint Identification System (IAFIS). This globally-deployed system is "always on" to help international, federal, state, and local law enforcement agencies to verify and validate evidence that has been submitted, to aide in properly identifying persons of interest (POI) or suspects, and bring them to justice in a court of law. IAFIS is the most comprehensive evidence-gathering electronic criminal fingerprint database in the world and can automatically access more than 70 million historical criminal records and histories, as well as a photo or "mugshot" of a suspect on file.

15. D: This piece of advanced technology is an imaging device that permits a laboratory technician to analyze ink (such as the ink on currency) in order to enable the human eye to see common hidden security features and potentially reveal evidence that a document or bill has been altered. This technology is used extensively in the effort to combat the worldwide black market of counterfeit currency.

Dear Private Investigator Test Taker,

We would like to start by thanking you for purchasing this study guide for your Private Investigator exam. We hope that we exceeded your expectations.

Our goal in creating this study guide was to cover all of the topics that you will see on the test. We also strove to make our practice questions as similar as possible to what you will encounter on test day. With that being said, if you found something that you feel was not up to your standards, please send us an email and let us know.

We would also like to let you know about this other book in our catalog that may interest you.

California POST

This can be found on Amazon: amazon.com/dp/1628459581

We have study guides in a wide variety of fields. If the one you are looking for isn't listed above, then try searching for it on Amazon or send us an email.

Thanks Again and Happy Testing!
Product Development Team
info@studyguideteam.com

FREE Test Taking Tips DVD Offer

To help us better serve you, we have developed a Test Taking Tips DVD that we would like to give you for FREE. **This DVD covers world-class test taking tips that you can use to be even more successful when you are taking your test.**

All that we ask is that you email us your feedback about your study guide. Please let us know what you thought about it – whether that is good, bad or indifferent.

To get your **FREE Test Taking Tips DVD**, email freedvd@studyguideteam.com with "FREE DVD" in the subject line and the following information in the body of the email:

      a. The title of your study guide.

      b. Your product rating on a scale of 1-5, with 5 being the highest rating.

      c. Your feedback about the study guide. What did you think of it?

      d. Your full name and shipping address to send your free DVD.

If you have any questions or concerns, please don't hesitate to contact us at freedvd@studyguideteam.com.

Thanks again!

Made in the USA
Las Vegas, NV
23 April 2023